THE
FATHER'S
ALMANAC

CRISWELL FREEMAN

FAMILY
Christian Stores®

The quoted ideas expressed in this book (but not scripture verses) are not, in all cases, exact quotations, as some have been edited for clarity and brevity. In all cases, the author has attempted to maintain the speaker's original intent. In some cases, quoted material for this book was obtained from secondary sources, primarily print media. While every effort was made to ensure the accuracy of these sources, the accuracy cannot be guaranteed. For additions, deletions, corrections or clarifications in future editions of this text, please write FAMILY CHRISTIAN STORES.

Cover Design by Kim Russell / Wahoo Designs
Page Layout by Bart Dawson

ISBN 978-1-60587-007-6

THE
FATHER'S
ALMANAC

CRISWELL FREEMAN

TABLE OF CONTENTS

INTRODUCTION

Because you're reading this book, you probably answer to the name Dad, Daddy, Pop, Father, or some variation thereof. If so, congratulations: few of life's joys can match the glorious responsibility of leading your family in the will and the Word of God.

In your hands you hold a handy almanac of great ideas for great dads like you. It contains essays, quotes, tips, Bible verses, and helpful hints that are intended to guide your path and lift your spirits.

As a dedicated dad, you know that parenting is hard work—lots of hard work. And as a Christian, you're also aware of another incalculable treasure that is yours for the asking: the gift of eternal life that was purchased by God's only begotten Son on the cross at Calvary. This book serves as an inspirational reminder of these and other blessings that you, as a Christian dad, can savor for a lifetime and beyond.

Fatherhood is both a priceless gift from God and an unrelenting responsibility. The ideas on these pages are intended to remind you that when it comes to the tough job of being a responsible father, you and God, working together, are destined to do great things for your kids and for the world.

CHAPTER 1

THANKS, DAD

The righteous man walks in his integrity;
His children are blessed after him.
PROVERBS 20:7 NKJV

Dear Dad,

Thanks for the love, for the work, for the care and discipline, for the wisdom, the support, and the faith. Thanks for being a godly man, a concerned parent, and a worthy example. Thanks for doing your best and never giving up, even when you were tired or frustrated—or both. Thanks for changing diapers and wiping away tears. And thanks for being a man worthy of our admiration and our love.

You deserve our thanks, Dad, but you deserve so much more. You deserve our family's undying gratitude. And, you deserve God's love, His grace, and His peace. That peace is yours through God's Son, Christ Jesus. May you accept God's blessings, not only for today, but also for all eternity.

Signed,

Your Family

MORE GREAT IDEAS ABOUT
FATHERS AND FAMILIES

How badly America needs husbands and fathers who are committed to their families, men who are determined to succeed in this important responsibility.

JAMES DOBSON

A man ought to live so that everybody knows he is a Christian, and most of all, his family ought to know.

D. L. MOODY

No other structure can replace the family. Without it, our children have no moral foundation. Without it, they become moral illiterates whose only law is self.

CHUCK COLSON

Real love has staying power. Authentic love is tough love. It refuses to look for ways to run away. It always opts for working through.

CHARLES SWINDOLL

The best use of life is love. The best expression of love is time. The best time to love is now.

RICK WARREN

As fathers, the greatest earthly gifts we can provide are our presence and influence while we live and a magnificent memory of our lives once we're gone.

CHARLES SWINDOLL

The father's most important responsibility is to communicate the real meaning of Christianity to his children.

JAMES DOBSON

I would rather be a nobody in the world, but be a somebody to my kids.

PATRICK MORLEY

My best training came from my father.

WOODROW WILSON

When the whole family is together, the soul is in place.

OLD-TIME PROVERB

MORE WISDOM FROM GOD'S WORD

The righteous one will live by his faith.

HABAKKUK 2:4 HCSB

And the world is passing away, and the lust of it; but he who does the will of God abides forever.

1 JOHN 2:17 NKJV

Because the eyes of the Lord are on the righteous and His ears are open to their request. But the face of the Lord is against those who do evil.

1 PETER 3:12 HCSB

Sow righteousness for yourselves and reap faithful love; break up your untilled ground. It is time to seek the Lord until He comes and sends righteousness on you like the rain.

HOSEA 10:12 HCSB

Choose for yourselves today the one you will worship . . . . As for me and my family, we will worship the Lord.

JOSHUA 24:15 HCSB

A FATHER'S WISH

I may fail to be as clever as my neighbor down the street,
I may fail to be as wealthy as some other men I meet,
I may never win the glory which a lot of men have had,
But I've got to be successful as a little fellow's dad.

There are certain dreams I cherish which I'd like to see
    come true,
There are things I would accomplish when my time of life
    is through,
But the task my heart is on is to guide a little lad
And to make myself successful as that little fellow's dad.

I may never come to glory, I may never gather gold,
Men may list me with the failures when my business life is
    told,
But if he who follows after shall be manly, I'll be glad,
For I'll know I've been successful as that little fellow's dad.

It's the one job that I dream of, it's the task I think of most,
If I fail that growing youngster, I'd have nothing else to
    boast;
For though wealth and fame I'd gathered, all my future
    would be sad . . .
If I failed to be successful as that little fellow's dad.

AUTHOR UNKNOWN

MORE GOOD IDEAS

It takes a heap of livin' in a house to make it home.

EDGAR A. GUEST

The happiest moments of my life have been the few which I have passed at home in the bosom of my family.

THOMAS JEFFERSON

Fathers are those who give daughters away to other men who aren't nearly good enough so they can have grandchildren who are smarter than anybody's.

PAUL HARVEY

A TIMELY TIP

Don't be too hard on yourself. You don't have to be a perfect parent to be a godly one. Do the best you can, and leave the rest up to God.

DEAR DAD,
On the Lines Below, Write Down Your Own Ideas About Being a Father

And Finally . . .

A father is someone
who carries pictures
where his money used to be.

CHAPTER 2

THE POWER OF PRAYER

The intense prayer of the righteous is very powerful.

—

JAMES 5:16 HCSB

This troubled world desperately needs your prayers, and so does your family. When you weave the habit of prayer into the very fabric of your day, you invite God to become a partner in every aspect of your life. When you consult God on an hourly basis, you avail yourself of His wisdom, His strength, and His love. And, because God answers prayers according to His perfect timetable, your petitions to Him will transform your family, your world, and yourself.

Today, turn everything over to your Creator in prayer. Instead of worrying about your next decision, decide to let God lead the way. Don't limit your prayers to meals or to bedtime. Pray constantly about things great and small. God is listening, and He wants to hear from you. Now.

MORE GREAT IDEAS ABOUT
PRAYER

It is well said that neglected prayer is the birth-place of all evil.

C. H. SPURGEON

Obedience is the master key to effective prayer.

BILLY GRAHAM

Prayer may not get us what we want, but it will teach us to want what we need.

VANCE HAVNER

Learn to pray to God in such a way that you are trusting Him as your Physician to do what He knows is best. Confess to Him the disease, and let Him choose the remedy.

ST. AUGUSTINE

Those who know God the best are the richest and most powerful in prayer. Little acquaintance with God, and strangeness and coldness to Him, make prayer a rare and feeble thing.

E. M. BOUNDS

My soul, hearken to the voice of your God. He is always ready to speak with you when you are prepared to hear. If there is any slowness to commune, it is not on His part but altogether on your own. He stands at the door and knocks, and if His people will only open, He rejoices to enter.

C. H. SPURGEON

God delights in the prayers of His children—prayers that express our love for Him, prayers that share our deepest burdens with Him.

BILLY GRAHAM

Pour out your heart to God and tell Him how you feel. Be real, be honest, and when you get it all out, you'll start to feel the gradual covering of God's comforting presence.

BILL HYBELS

All children have the right to a daddy . . . rational and sound and showing his love by the way he treats them.

JERRY CLOWER

One father is more than a hundred school masters.

OLD-TIME PROVERB

MORE WISDOM FROM GOD'S WORD

Rejoice in hope; be patient in affliction; be persistent in prayer.

ROMANS 12:12 HCSB

Let the words of my mouth and the meditation of my heart be acceptable in Your sight, O Lord, my strength and my Redeemer.

PSALM 19:14 NKJV

Yet He often withdrew to deserted places and prayed.

LUKE 5:16 HCSB

Don't worry about anything, but in everything, through prayer and petition with thanksgiving, let your requests be made known to God.

PHILIPPIANS 4:6 HCSB

The Lord is far from the wicked but he hears the prayer of the righteous.

PROVERBS 15:29 NIV

ASK GOD FOR THE THINGS YOU NEED

Sometimes, amid the demands and the frustrations of everyday life, we forget to slow ourselves down long enough to talk with God. Instead of turning our thoughts and prayers to Him, we rely upon our own resources. Instead of praying for strength and courage, we seek to manufacture it within ourselves. Instead of asking God for guidance, we depend only upon our own limited wisdom. The results of such behaviors are unfortunate and, on occasion, tragic.

Are you in need? Ask God to sustain you. Are you troubled? Take your worries to Him in prayer. Are you weary? Seek God's strength. In all things great and small, seek God's wisdom and His grace. He hears your prayers, and He will answer. All you must do is ask.

MORE GOOD IDEAS

All we have to do is to acknowledge our need, move from self-sufficiency to dependence, and ask God to become our hiding place.

BILL HYBELS

Some people think God does not like to be troubled with our constant asking. But, the way to trouble God is not to come at all.

D. L. MOODY

Don't be afraid to ask your heavenly Father for anything you need. Indeed, nothing is too small for God's attention or too great for his power.

DENNIS SWANBERG

A TIMELY TIP

Pray early and often. God is listening, and your children are watching.

DEAR DAD,
On the Lines Below, Write Down Your Own Ideas About The Power of Prayer

AND FINALLY . . .

DID YOU KNOW?

Sonora Louise Smart Dodd, of Spokane, Washington, began the tradition of Father's Day in 1910 in honor of her dad.

CHAPTER 3

FATHERS WHO LOVE

We love because He first loved us.

—

1 JOHN 4:19 HCSB

As a caring father, you understand the deep love that you feel for your family. And, you know the impact that your feelings can have upon your loved ones: few things in life are as precious or enduring as a father's love.

The familiar words of 1st Corinthians 13 remind us that love is God's commandment. Faith is important, of course. So, too, is hope. But love is more important still.

Christ demonstrated His love for us on the cross, and, as Christians, we are called upon to return Christ's love by sharing it. We are to love one another just as Christ loved us (John 13:34). That's a tall order, but as believers, we are obligated to follow it. And as fathers, we are obligated to love our families just as our Heavenly Father first loved us.

MORE GREAT IDEAS ABOUT LOVE

Love must be supported and fed and protected, just like a little infant who is growing up at home.

JAMES DOBSON

Beware that you are not swallowed up in books! An ounce of love is worth a pound of knowledge.

JOHN WESLEY

Brotherly love is still the distinguishing badge of every true Christian.

MATTHEW HENRY

Love is not measured by what it gets, but by what it costs.

OSWALD CHAMBERS

Forgiveness is the final form of love.

REINHOLD NIEBUHR

The truth of the Gospel is intended to free us to love God and others with our whole heart.

JOHN ELDREDGE

How do you spell love? When you reach the point where the happiness, security, and development of another person is as much of a driving force to you as your own happiness, security, and development, then you have a mature love. True love is spelled G-I-V-E. It is not based on what you can get, but rooted in what you can give to the other person.

JOSH MCDOWELL

Truth becomes hard if it is not softened by love, and love becomes soft if not strengthened by truth.

E. STANLEY JONES

Live your lives in love, the same sort of love which Christ gives us, and which He perfectly expressed when He gave Himself as a sacrifice to God.

CORRIE TEN BOOM

You will find, as you look back upon your life, that the moments when you have really lived are the moments when you have done things in the spirit of love.

HENRY DRUMMOND

MORE WISDOM FROM GOD'S WORD

I pray that you, being rooted and firmly established in love, may be able to comprehend with all the saints what is the breadth and width, height and depth, and to know the Messiah's love that surpasses knowledge, so you may be filled with all the fullness of God.

EPHESIANS 3:17-19 HCSB

If I speak the languages of men and of angels, but do not have love, I am a sounding gong or a clanging cymbal.

1 CORINTHIANS 13:1 HCSB

Now these three remain: faith, hope, and love. But the greatest of these is love.

1 CORINTHIANS 13:13 HCSB

Dear friends, if God loved us in this way, we also must love one another.

1 JOHN 4:11 HCSB

Mighty waters cannot extinguish love; rivers cannot sweep it away.

SONG OF SOLOMON 8:7 HCSB

On Loving and Listening

For many parents, the temptation to lecture their children is almost irresistible. But oftentimes, it's more helpful to listen than to lecture.

God's Word instructs us to be quick to listen and slow to speak. And when it comes to the important job of raising the next generation and strengthening our families, we're wise to listen carefully (first) and then offer helpful words (next).

Perhaps God gave us two ears and one mouth for a reason: so that we might listen twice as much as we speak. After all, listening quietly to our kids can be a wonderful form of encouragement. Besides, after we've listened carefully to our youngsters, we're more likely to respond wisely, not impulsively.

So remember that, as a parent, you have the power to guide your child with your words and your ears. And remember that the words you don't speak can be just as helpful as the ones you do speak. So talk—and listen—accordingly.

MORE GOOD IDEAS

Listening is loving.

ZIG ZIGLAR

The failure to listen might be the biggest hindrance of all to family communications.

ED YOUNG

The cliché is true: People don't care what we know until they know we care.

RICK WARREN

A TIMELY TIP

The kids are watching: Your children form their ideas about God's love by experiencing their parents' love. Live—and love—accordingly.

DEAR DAD,
On the Lines Below, Write Down Your Own Ideas About Love

AND FINALLY . . .

DID YOU KNOW?

In 1916, U.S. President Woodrow Wilson approved the idea of observing an annual Father's Day.

CHAPTER 4

THE RIGHT KIND OF EXAMPLE

Set an example of good works yourself,
with integrity and dignity in your teaching.

—

—TITUS 2:7 HCSB

Our children learn from the lessons we teach and the lives we live, but not necessarily in that order. As fathers, we serve as unforgettable role models for our children and our grandchildren. The lives we lead and the choices we make should serve as enduring examples of the spiritual abundance that is available to all who worship God and obey His commandments.

Are you God's obedient servant? Is your faith in Christ clearly demonstrated by the example that you set for your children? If so, you will be blessed by God, and so, of course, will they.

MORE GREAT IDEAS ABOUT
SETTING A GOOD EXAMPLE

If we have the true love of God in our hearts, we will show it in our lives. We will not have to go up and down the earth proclaiming it. We will show it in everything we say or do.

D. L. MOODY

Integrity of heart is indispensable.

JOHN CALVIN

There is no way to grow a saint overnight. Character, like the oak tree, does not spring up like a mushroom.

VANCE HAVNER

The sermon of your life in tough times ministers to people more powerfully than the most eloquent speaker.

BILL BRIGHT

What we practice, not (save at rare intervals) what we preach, is usually our great contribution to the conversion of others.

C. S. LEWIS

The Holy Spirit was given to guide us into all truth, but He doesn't do it all at once.

ELISABETH ELLIOT

The best evidence of our having the truth is our walking in the truth.

MATTHEW HENRY

Having a doctrine pass before the mind is not what the Bible means by knowing the truth. It's only when it reaches down deep into the heart that the truth begins to set us free, just as a key must penetrate a lock to turn it, or as rainfall must saturate the earth down to the roots in order for your garden to grow.

JOHN ELDREDGE

A person who lives right, and is right, has more power in his silence than another has by words.

PHILLIPS BROOKS

A child identifies his parents with God, whether adults want the role or not. Most children "see" God the way they perceive their earthly fathers.

JAMES DOBSON

MORE WISDOM FROM GOD'S WORD

For the kingdom of God is not in talk but in power.

1 CORINTHIANS 4:20 HCSB

Therefore since we also have such a large cloud of witnesses surrounding us, let us lay aside every weight and the sin that so easily ensnares us, and run with endurance the race that lies before us.

HEBREWS 12:1 HCSB

You should be an example to the believers in speech, in conduct, in love, in faith, in purity.

1 TIMOTHY 4:12 HCSB

Do everything without grumbling and arguing, so that you may be blameless and pure.

PHILIPPIANS 2:14–15 HCSB

For you were once darkness, but now you are light in the Lord. Walk as children of light—for the fruit of the light results in all goodness, righteousness, and truth—discerning what is pleasing to the Lord.

EPHESIANS 5:8-10 HCSB

MORE GOOD IDEAS

Example is not the main thing in influencing others—it is the only thing.

ALBERT SCHWEITZER

None preaches better than the ant, and he says nothing.

BEN FRANKLIN

I'd rather see a sermon than hear one any day; I'd rather one should walk with me than merely tell the way.

EDGAR A. GUEST

A TIMELY TIP

Calling all parents! What the world needs is more parents who are willing to be positive role models to their children. God wants you to be that kind of parent . . . now!

DEAR DAD,
On the Lines Below, Write Down Your Own Ideas About Setting the Right Kind of Example

CHAPTER 5

THE POWER OF ENCOURAGEMENT

Anxiety in a man's heart weighs it down,
but a good word cheers it up.

—

Every member of your family needs a regular supply of encouraging words and pats on the back. And you need the rewards that God gives to those enthusiastic dads who are a continual source of encouragement to their wives and children.

In his letter to the Ephesians, Paul writes, "Do not let any unwholesome talk come out of your mouths, but only what is helpful for building others up according to their needs, that it may benefit those who listen" (4:29 NIV). This passage reminds us that, as Christians, we are instructed to choose our words carefully so as to build others up through wholesome, honest encouragement. How can we build others up? By celebrating their victories and their accomplishments. As the old saying goes, "When someone does something good, applaud—you'll make two people happy."

Today, look for the good in others—starting with your family. And then, celebrate the good that you find. When you do, you'll be a powerful force of encouragement in the world . . . and a worthy servant to your God.

MORE GREAT IDEAS ABOUT ENCOURAGEMENT

We have the Lord, but He Himself has recognized that we need the touch of a human hand. He Himself came down and lived among us as a man. We cannot see Him now, but blessed be the tie that binds human hearts in Christian love.

VANCE HAVNER

The truest help we can render an afflicted man is not to take his burden from him, but to call out his best energy, that he may be able to bear the burden himself.

PHILLIPS BROOKS

God grant that we may not hinder those who are battling their way slowly into the light.

OSWALD CHAMBERS

You can't light another's path without casting light on your own.

JOHN MAXWELL

It is helpful to remember the distinction between appreciation and affirmation. We appreciate what a person does, but we affirm who a person is.

CHARLES SWINDOLL

A lot of people have gone further than they thought they could because someone else thought they could.

ZIG ZIGLAR

I can usually sense that a leading is from the Holy Spirit when it calls me to humble myself, to serve somebody, to encourage somebody, or to give something away. Very rarely will the evil one lead us to do those kind of things.

BILL HYBELS

Friendships are living organisms at work. They continue to unfold, change, and emerge.

BARBARA JOHNSON

In each of my friends there is something that only some other friend can fully bring out. By myself I am not large enough to call the whole man into activity; I want other lights than my own to show all his facets.

C. S. LEWIS

MORE WISDOM FROM GOD'S WORD

I want their hearts to be encouraged and joined together in love, so that they may have all the riches of assured understanding, and have the knowledge of God's mystery—Christ.

COLOSSIANS 2:2 HCSB

Carry one another's burdens; in this way you will fulfill the law of Christ.

GALATIANS 6:2 HCSB

But encourage each other daily, while it is still called today, so that none of you is hardened by sin's deception.

HEBREWS 3:13 HCSB

And let us be concerned about one another in order to promote love and good works.

HEBREWS 10:24 HCSB

Therefore encourage one another and build each other up as you are already doing.

1 THESSALONIANS 5:11 HCSB

THE POWER OF GENUINE FRIENDSHIP

What is a friend? The dictionary defines the word "friend" as "a person who is attached to another by feelings of affection or personal regard." This definition is accurate, as far as it goes, but when we examine the deeper meaning of friendship, so many more descriptors come to mind: trustworthiness, loyalty, helpfulness, kindness, understanding, forgiveness, encouragement, humor, and cheerfulness, to mention but a few.

Genuine friendship should be treasured and nourished. As Christians, we are governed by the Golden Rule: we are commanded to treat others as we wish to be treated. When we treat others with kindness, courtesy, and respect, we build friendships that can last a lifetime. And God smiles.

43

MORE GOOD IDEAS

Nothing opens the heart like a true friend, to whom you may impart griefs, joys, fears, hopes, suspicions, counsels, and whatever lies upon the heart.

FRANCIS BACON

The glory of friendship is not the outstretched hand, or the kindly smile, or the joy of companionship. It is the spiritual inspiration that comes to one when he discovers that someone else believes in him and is willing to trust him with his friendship.

CORRIE TEN BOOM

A TIMELY TIP

You know that your child is a unique gift from God . . . make sure that your child hears that message every day . . . from you.

DEAR DAD,
On the Lines Below, Write Down Your Own Ideas About The Power of Encouragement

AND FINALLY . . .

THE BEST WAY TO KNOCK
THE CHIP OFF YOUR NEIGHBOR'S
SHOULDER IS TO PAT HIM ON THE BACK.

CHAPTER 6

FATHERS WHO WORK DILIGENTLY

Whatever you do, do it enthusiastically,
as something done for the Lord and not for men.

—

COLOSSIANS 3:23 HCSB

Providing for your family requires work and lots of it. And as a hardworking dad, you have earned the gratitude of your loved ones and the praise of your Heavenly Father.

It has been said that there are no shortcuts to anyplace worth going. Dads agree. Making the grade in today's competitive workplace is not easy. In fact, it can be very difficult indeed. But, even when the workday is long and the workload is difficult, we must not become discouraged.

God did not create us for lives of mediocrity; He created us for far greater things. Earning great things usually requires determination, persistence, and hard work—which is perfectly fine with God. After all, He knows that we're up to the task, and He has big plans for us. Very big plans . . .

MORE GREAT IDEAS ABOUT
WORK

Thank God every morning when you get up that you have something which must be done, whether you like it or not. Work breeds a hundred virtues that idleness never knows.

CHARLES KINGSLEY

It may be that the day of judgment will dawn tomorrow; in that case, we shall gladly stop working for a better tomorrow. But not before.

DIETRICH BONHOEFFER

The world does not consider labor a blessing, therefore it flees and hates it, but the pious who fear the Lord labor with a ready and cheerful heart, for they know God's command, and they acknowledge His calling.

MARTIN LUTHER

If, in your working hours, you make the work your end, you will presently find yourself all unawares inside the only circle in your profession that really matters. You will be one of the sound craftsmen, and other sound craftsmen will know it.

C. S. LEWIS

Few things fire up a person's commitment like dedication to excellence.

JOHN MAXWELL

Freedom is not an absence of responsibility; but rather a reward we receive when we've performed our responsibility with excellence.

CHARLES SWINDOLL

When we wholeheartedly commit ourselves to God, there is nothing mediocre or run-of-the-mill about us. To live for Christ is to be passionate about our Lord and about our lives.

JIM GALLERY

Making up a string of excuses is usually harder than doing the work.

MARIE T. FREEMAN

Don't take hold of a thing unless you want that thing to take hold of you.

E. STANLEY JONES

MORE WISDOM FROM GOD'S WORD

Whatever your hands find to do, do with [all] your strength.

ECCLESIASTES 9:10 HCSB

He did it with all his heart. So he prospered.

2 CHRONICLES 31:21 NKJV

Don't work only while being watched, in order to please men, but as slaves of Christ, do God's will from your heart. Render service with a good attitude, as to the Lord and not to men.

EPHESIANS 6:6-7 HCSB

We must do the works of Him who sent Me while it is day. Night is coming when no one can work.

JOHN 9:4 HCSB

The people had a mind to work.

NEHEMIAH 4:6 KJV

IN SEARCH OF EXCELLENCE

How does God intend for us to work? Does He intend for us to work diligently or does He, instead, reward mediocrity? The answer is obvious. God has created a world in which hard work is rewarded and sloppy work is not. Yet sometimes, we may seek ease over excellence, or we may be tempted to take shortcuts when God intends that we walk the straight and narrow path.

Today, heed God's Word by doing good work. Wherever you find yourself, whatever your job description, do your work, and do it with all your heart. When you do, you will most certainly win the recognition of your peers. But more importantly, God will bless your efforts and use you in ways that only He can understand. So do your work with focus and dedication. And leave the rest up to God.

MORE GOOD IDEAS

The quality of a person's life is in direct proportion to his commitment to excellence, regardless of his chosen field of endeavor.

VINCE LOMBARDI

When it becomes necessary to do a thing, the whole heart and soul should go into the measure, or not attempt it.

THOMAS PAINE

A TIMELY TIP

Wherever you happen to be, be the best you can be. Excellence is habit-forming, so give your best every time you go to work. And if you haven't yet found the high-paying job of your dreams, don't make the mistake of thinking that you can get by with pint-sized productivity. Whatever your job, whether you're the hall-of-fame head coach or the wet-behind-the-ears water boy, behave yourself like a winner by doing your work with care, with pride, and with enthusiasm.

DEAR DAD,
On the Lines Below, Write Down Your Own Ideas About The Rewards of Hard Work

AND FINALLY . . .

Diligence is the mother of good luck,
and God gives all things to industry.
Then plough deep while sluggards sleep,
and you shall have corn to sell and to keep.

—

POOR RICHARD'S ALMANAC

CHAPTER 7

FATHERS WHO MODEL DISCIPLINE

*No discipline seems enjoyable at the time, but painful.
Later on, however, it yields the fruit of peace
and righteousness to those who have been trained by it.*

—

HEBREWS 12:11 HCSB

A re you a self-disciplined dad? If so, congratulations . . . if not, God wants to have a little talk with you.

You live in a world in which leisure is glorified and indifference is often glamorized. But God has other plans. He did not create you to be ordinary; He created you for far greater things.

Life's greatest rewards aren't likely to fall into your lap. To the contrary, your greatest accomplishments will probably require lots of work, which is perfectly fine with God. After all, He knows that you're up to the task, and He has big plans for you. God will do His part to fulfill those plans, and the rest, of course, is up to you.

Now, are you steadfast in your determination to be a self-disciplined man? If so, pat yourself on the back . . . if not, reread this little essay—and keep reading it—until God's message finally sinks in.

MORE GREAT IDEAS ABOUT
DISCIPLINE

The Bible calls for discipline and a recognition of authority. Children must learn this at home.

BILLY GRAHAM

Discipline is training that develops and corrects.

CHARLES STANLEY

Work is doing it. Discipline is doing it every day. Diligence is doing it well every day.

DAVE RAMSEY

God cannot build character without our cooperation. If we resist Him, then He chastens us into submission. But, if we submit to Him, then He can accomplish His work. He is not satisfied with a halfway job. God wants a perfect work; He wants a finished product that is mature and complete.

WARREN WIERSBE

Personal humility is a spiritual discipline and the hallmark of the service of Jesus.

FRANKLIN GRAHAM

As we seek to become disciples of Jesus Christ, we should never forget that the word *disciple* is directly related to the word *discipline*. To be a disciple of the Lord Jesus Christ is to know his discipline.

DENNIS SWANBERG

The alternative to discipline is disaster.

VANCE HAVNER

If one examines the secret behind a championship football team, a magnificent orchestra, or a successful business, the principal ingredient is invariably discipline.

JAMES DOBSON

Any man's life will be filled with constant and unexpected encouragement if he makes up his mind to do his level best each day.

BOOKER T. WASHINGTON

In reading the lives of great men, I found that the first victory they won was over themselves: with all of them, self-discipline came first.

HARRY TRUMAN

MORE WISDOM FROM GOD'S WORD

The one who follows instruction is on the path to life, but the one who rejects correction goes astray.

PROVERBS 10:17 HCSB

For this very reason, make every effort to supplement your faith with goodness, goodness with knowledge, knowledge with self-control, self-control with endurance, endurance with godliness.

2 PETER 1:5-6 HCSB

I discipline my body and bring it under strict control, so that after preaching to others, I myself will not be disqualified.

1 CORINTHIANS 9:27 HCSB

Therefore by their fruits you will know them.

MATTHEW 7:20 NKJV

But each person should examine his own work, and then he will have a reason for boasting in himself alone, and not in respect to someone else. For each person will have to carry his own load.

GALATIANS 6:4-5 HCSB

MORE GOOD IDEAS

Without self-discipline, success is impossible. Period.

LOU HOLTZ

I've never known a man worth his salt who, in the long run, deep down in his heart, didn't appreciate the grind, the discipline. I firmly believe that any man's finest hour, this greatest fulfillment to all he holds dear, is that moment he has worked his heart out in a good cause and lies exhausted on the field of battle, victorious.

VINCE LOMBARDI

No man is fit to command another that cannot command himself.

WILLIAM PENN

A TIMELY TIP

Take a disciplined approach to disciplining your child: If you're too angry for your own good, put yourself in time-out until you can control yourself.

DEAR DAD,
On the Lines Below, Write Down Your Own Ideas About
The Rewards of Discipline

CHAPTER 8

FATHERS WHO LEAD THEIR FAMILIES

---

*According to the grace given to us, we have different gifts:
If prophecy, use it according to the standard of faith; if service,
in service; if teaching, in teaching; if exhorting,
in exhortation; giving, with generosity; leading, with diligence;
showing mercy, with cheerfulness.*

—

ROMANS 12:6-8 HCSB

As the leader of your family, you have a profound responsibility to your loved ones and to your God. If you desire to be an obedient servant to your Heavenly Father, you must lead your family according to His Holy Word. To do otherwise is to rob your loved ones of the peace and abundance that is rightfully theirs through the person of Jesus Christ.

Our world needs Christian leaders, and so does your family. So make this pledge and keep it: vow to become the godly leader that God intends you to be. Your family needs you, and you need the experience of leading them in the service of our Lord.

MORE GREAT IDEAS ABOUT LEADERSHIP

You can never separate a leader's actions from his character.

JOHN MAXWELL

A man ought to live so that everybody knows he is a Christian, and most of all, his family ought to know.

D. L. MOODY

A wise leader chooses a variety of gifted individuals. He complements his strengths.

CHARLES STANLEY

What do we Christians chiefly value in our leaders? The answer seems to be not their holiness, but their gifts and skills and resources. The thought that only holy people are likely to be spiritually useful does not loom large in our minds.

J. I. PACKER

Integrity and maturity are two character traits vital to the heart of a leader.

CHARLES STANLEY

A true and safe leader is likely to be one who has no desire to lead, but is forced into a position of leadership by inward pressure of the Holy Spirit and the press of external situation.

A. W. TOZER

Leaders must learn how to wait. Often their followers don't always see as far as they see or have the faith that they have.

WARREN WIERSBE

The test of a leader is taking the vision from me to we.

JOHN MAXWELL

Enthusiasm invites enthusiasm.

RUSSELL CONWELL

Effective leadership is putting first things first. Effective management is discipline, carrying it out.

STEPHEN COVEY

MORE WISDOM FROM GOD'S WORD

Shepherd God's flock among you, not overseeing out of compulsion but freely, according to God's will; not for the money but eagerly.

1 PETER 5:2 HCSB

And we exhort you, brothers: warn those who are lazy, comfort the discouraged, help the weak, be patient with everyone.

1 THESSALONIANS 5:14 HCSB

An overseer, therefore, must be above reproach, the husband of one wife, self-controlled, sensible, respectable, hospitable, an able teacher, not addicted to wine, not a bully but gentle, not quarrelsome, not greedy.

1 TIMOTHY 3:2-3 HCSB

His master said to him, "Well done, good and faithful slave! You were faithful over a few things; I will put you in charge of many things. Enter your master's joy!"

MATTHEW 25:21 HCSB

So then, we must pursue what promotes peace and what builds up one another.

ROMANS 14:19 HCSB

MORE GOOD IDEAS

Leadership begins with self-knowledge. Life decisions can be good decisions only if they reflect your own personal bedrock.

VINCE LOMBARDI

I never tell my players anything I don't absolutely believe myself.

VINCE LOMBARDI

Confidence is contagious. So is lack of confidence.

VINCE LOMBARDI

A TIMELY TIP

In thinking about your leadership style, ask yourself this: who's your model? If you're wise, you'll try, as best you can, to emulate Jesus.

DEAR DAD,
On the Lines Below, Write Down Your Own Ideas About
Effective Leadership

CHAPTER 9

THE IMPORTANCE OF CHARACTER

People with integrity have firm footing,
but those who follow crooked paths will slip and fall.

—

PROVERBS 10:9 NLT

Charles Swindoll correctly observed, "Nothing speaks louder or more powerfully than a life of integrity." Wise dads agree.

Character is built slowly over a lifetime. It is the sum of every right decision, every honest word, every noble thought, and every heartfelt prayer. It is forged on the anvil of honorable work and polished by the twin virtues of generosity and humility. Character is a precious thing— difficult to build but easy to tear down. As believers in Christ, we must seek to live each day with discipline, honesty, and faith. When we do, integrity becomes a habit.

If you sincerely wish to be a righteous man, then you must walk with God and you must follow His commandments. When you do, your character will take care of itself . . . and God will surely smile upon you and yours.

MORE GREAT IDEAS ABOUT
CHARACTER

There is something about having endured great loss that brings purity of purpose and strength of character.

BARBARA JOHNSON

Often, our character is at greater risk in prosperity than in adversity.

BETH MOORE

We actually are, at present, creatures whose character must be, in some respects, a horror to God, as it is, when we really see it, a horror to ourselves. This I believe to be a fact: and I notice that the holier a man is, the more fully he is aware of that fact.

C. S. LEWIS

Each one of us is God's special work of art. Through us, He teaches and inspires, delights and encourages, informs and uplifts all those who view our lives. God, the master artist, is most concerned about expressing Himself—His thoughts and His intentions—through what He paints in our characters.

JONI EARECKSON TADA

Integrity is the glue that holds our way of life together. We must constantly strive to keep our integrity intact. When wealth is lost, nothing is lost; when health is lost, something is lost; when character is lost, all is lost.

BILLY GRAHAM

Integrity is not a given factor in everyone's life. It is a result of self-discipline, inner trust, and a decision to be relentlessly honest in all situations in our lives.

JOHN MAXWELL

Honesty has a beautiful and refreshing simplicity about it. No ulterior motives. No hidden meanings. As honesty and integrity characterize our lives, there will be no need to manipulate others.

CHARLES SWINDOLL

The single most important element in any human relationship is honesty—with oneself, with God, and with others.

CATHERINE MARSHALL

In matters of principle, stand like a rock.

THOMAS JEFFERSON

MORE WISDOM FROM GOD'S WORD

Do not be misled: "Bad company corrupts good character."

1 CORINTHIANS 15:33 NIV

Applying all diligence, in your faith supply moral excellence.

2 PETER 1:5 NASB

The righteousness of the blameless clears his path, but the wicked person will fall because of his wickedness.

PROVERBS 11:5 HCSB

A good name is more desirable than great riches; to be esteemed is better than silver or gold.

PROVERBS 22:1 NIV

Good people's words will help many others.

PROVERBS 10:21 NCV

LISTENING TO YOUR CONSCIENCE

Few things in life provide more comfort than a clear conscience. In fact, a clear conscience is one of the undeniable blessings that you earn whenever you allow God to guide your path through the trials and temptations of everyday life.

Have you formed the habit of listening carefully to that little voice inside your head? And when you hear what your conscience has to say, do you behave yourself accordingly? Hopefully so, because that little voice has much to teach you about the choices you decide to make and the life you decide to live. So today, as you make countless choices about the things you do and the things you say, let your conscience be your guide. When you do, you'll never stay lost for long.

MORE GOOD IDEAS

An honest heart is the first blessing. A knowing heart is the second.

THOMAS JEFFERSON

Let your tongue speak what your heart thinks.

DAVY CROCKETT

The most enviable of all titles: an honest man.

GEORGE WASHINGTON

A TIMELY TIP

The more important the decision . . . the more carefully you should listen to your conscience.

DEAR DAD,
On the Lines Below, Write Down Your Own Ideas About The Importance of Integrity

AND FINALLY . . .

If the rascals knew the advantage of virtue,
they would become honest men.

—

POOR RICHARD'S ALMANAC

CHAPTER 10

THIS IS THE DAY

This is the day the LORD has made;
we will rejoice and be glad in it.

—

PSALM 118:24 NKJV

Life is God's gift to you, and He intends that you celebrate His glorious gift. If you're a dad who treasures each day—and if you teach your children to do the same—you will be blessed by your Father in heaven.

For Christian believers, every day begins and ends with God and His Son. Christ came to this earth to give us abundant life and eternal salvation. Our task is to accept Christ's grace with joy in our hearts and praise on our lips. Believers who fashion their days around Jesus are transformed: They see the world differently, they act differently, and they feel differently about themselves and their neighbors.

Christians face the inevitable challenges and disappointments of each day armed with the joy of Christ and the promise of salvation. So whatever this day holds for you, begin it and end it with God as your partner and Christ as your Savior. And throughout the day, give thanks to the One who created you and saved you. God's love for you is infinite. Accept it joyously and be thankful.

MORE GREAT IDEAS ABOUT
CELEBRATION

A child of God should be a visible beatitude for joy and a living doxology for gratitude.

C. H. SPURGEON

Joy is the direct result of having God's perspective on our daily lives and the effect of loving our Lord enough to obey His commands and trust His promises.

BILL BRIGHT

Our sense of joy, satisfaction, and fulfillment in life increases, no matter what the circumstances, if we are in the center of God's will.

BILLY GRAHAM

A life of intimacy with God is characterized by joy.

OSWALD CHAMBERS

When we get rid of inner conflicts and wrong attitudes toward life, we will almost automatically burst into joy.

E. STANLEY JONES

Our thoughts, not our circumstances, determine our happiness.

JOHN MAXWELL

Some of us seem so anxious about avoiding hell that we forget to celebrate our journey toward heaven.

PHILIP YANCEY

We act as though comfort and luxury were the chief requirements of life, when all we need to make us really happy is something to be enthusiastic about.

CHARLES KINGSLEY

If you can forgive the person you were, accept the person you are, and believe in the person you will become, you are headed for joy. So celebrate your life.

BARBARA JOHNSON

Christ is the secret, the source, the substance, the center, and the circumference of all true and lasting gladness.

MRS. CHARLES E. COWMAN

MORE WISDOM FROM GOD'S WORD

Rejoice in the Lord always. I will say it again: Rejoice!

PHILIPPIANS 4:4 HCSB

David and the whole house of Israel were celebrating before the Lord.

2 SAMUEL 6:5 HCSB

Their sorrow was turned into rejoicing and their mourning into a holiday. They were to be days of feasting, rejoicing, and of sending gifts to one another and the poor.

ESTHER 9:22 HCSB

At the dedication of the wall of Jerusalem, they sent for the Levites wherever they lived and brought them to Jerusalem to celebrate the joyous dedication with thanksgiving and singing accompanied by cymbals, harps, and lyres.

NEHEMIAH 12:27 HCSB

If they serve Him obediently, they will end their days in prosperity and their years in happiness.

JOB 36:11 HCSB

HOW TO BE HAPPY

Happiness depends less upon our circumstances than upon our thoughts. When we turn our thoughts to God, to His gifts, and to His glorious creation, we experience the joy that God intends for His children. But, when we focus on the negative aspects of life, we inadvertently bring needless pain to our friends, to our families, and to ourselves.

Do you sincerely want to be a happy person? Then set your mind and your heart upon God's love and His grace. Seek a genuine, intimate, life-altering relationship with your Creator by studying His Word and trusting His promises. And while you're at it, count your blessings instead of your hardships. Then, after you've done these things, claim the joy, the peace, and the spiritual abundance that the Shepherd offers His sheep.

MORE GOOD IDEAS

Happiness, like its opposite, is habit-forming.

JIM GALLERY

Joy cannot be pursued. It comes from within. It is a state of being. It does not depend on circumstances, but triumphs over circumstances. It produces a gentleness of spirit and a magnetic personality.

BILLY GRAHAM

Joy comes not from what we have but from what we are.

C. H. SPURGEON

A TIMELY TIP

Every day is a glorious opportunity to place yourself in the service of the One who is the Giver of all blessings. When you celebrate God's gifts—when you place God's promises firmly in your mind and your heart—you'll find yourself celebrating life. And that, by the way, is exactly what God wants you to do.

DEAR DAD,

On the Lines Below, Write Down Your Own Ideas About
The Need to Celebrate Life

_____

_____

_____

_____

_____

_____

_____

_____

_____

_____

_____

_____

_____

_____

_____

_____

_____

_____

_____

_____

_____

AND FINALLY . . .

SMILE . . .
IT INCREASES YOUR FACE VALUE.

CHAPTER 11

PRAISING GOD EVERY DAY

Praise the Lord, all nations! Glorify Him, all peoples!
For great is His faithful love to us;
the Lord's faithfulness endures forever. Hallelujah!

—

PSALM 117 HCSB

God has given you gifts that are beyond measure. He sent His only begotten Son to die for you, and He gave you a family to care for and to love. God has given you another day of life, and He has filled it to the brim with opportunities to celebrate and to serve. What should you do in return for God's priceless gifts? You should praise Him always.

Today, as you travel to work, as you hug your child or kiss your spouse, as you gaze upon a passing cloud or marvel at a glorious sunset, think of what God has done for you, for yours, and for all of us. And, every time you notice a gift from the Giver of all things good, praise Him. His works are marvelous, His gifts are beyond understanding, and His love endures forever.

MORE GREAT IDEAS ABOUT
PRAISE

The words "thank" and "think" come from the same root word. If we would think more, we would thank more.

WARREN WIERSBE

A child of God should be a visible beatitude for joy and a living doxology for gratitude.

C. H. SPURGEON

Why wait until the fourth Thursday in November? Why wait until the morning of December twenty-fifth? Thanksgiving to God should be an everyday affair. The time to be thankful is now!

JIM GALLERY

Praise reestablishes the proper chain of command; we recognize that the King is on the throne and that he has saved his people.

MAX LUCADO

It is only with gratitude that life becomes rich.

DIETRICH BONHOEFFER

Thank God every morning when you get up that you have something to do that day which must be done, whether you like it or not.

CHARLES KINGSLEY

Holy, holy, holy! Lord God Almighty! All Thy works shall praise Thy name in earth, and sky, and sea.

REGINALD HEBER

Praise is the highest occupation of any being.

MAX LUCADO

Thanksgiving or complaining—these words express two contrastive attitudes of the souls of God's children in regard to His dealings with them. The soul that gives thanks can find comfort in everything; the soul that complains can find comfort in nothing.

HANNAH WHITALL SMITH

It is always possible to be thankful for what is given rather than to complain about what is not given. One or the other becomes a habit of life.

ELISABETH ELLIOT

MORE WISDOM FROM GOD'S WORD

But I will hope continually and will praise You more and more.

PSALM 71:14 HCSB

Therefore, through Him let us continually offer up to God a sacrifice of praise, that is, the fruit of our lips that confess His name.

HEBREWS 13:15 HCSB

So that at the name of Jesus every knee should bow—of those who are in heaven and on earth and under the earth—and every tongue should confess that Jesus Christ is Lord, to the glory of God the Father.

PHILIPPIANS 2:10-11 HCSB

Enter into his gates with thanksgiving, and into his courts with praise: be thankful unto him, and bless his name. For the LORD is good; his mercy is everlasting; and his truth endureth to all generations.

PSALM 100:4-5 KJV

And suddenly there was with the angel a multitude of the heavenly host praising God and saying: "Glory to God in the highest, And on earth peace, goodwill toward men!"

LUKE 2:13-14 NKJV

BE THANKFUL!

God's Word makes it clear: a wise heart is a thankful heart. Period. We are to worship God, in part, by the genuine gratitude we feel in our hearts for the marvelous blessings that our Creator has bestowed upon us. Yet even the most saintly among us must endure periods of bitterness, fear, doubt, and regret. Why? Because we are imperfect human beings who are incapable of perfect gratitude. Still, even on life's darker days, we must seek to cleanse our hearts of negative emotions and fill them, instead, with praise, with love, with hope, and with thanksgiving. To do otherwise is to be unfair to ourselves, to our loved ones, and to our God.

MORE GOOD IDEAS

The act of thanksgiving is a demonstration of the fact that you are going to trust and believe God.

KAY ARTHUR

The joy of the Holy Spirit is experienced by giving thanks in all situations.

BILL BRIGHT

God has promised that if we harvest well with the tools of thanksgiving, there will be seeds for planting in the spring.

GLORIA GAITHER

A TIMELY TIP

When you pray, don't just ask God for things—also take time to praise Him.

DEAR DAD,
On the Lines Below, Write Down Your Own Ideas About Your Reasons for Praising God

AND FINALLY . . .

DID YOU KNOW?

In the United States, there are
more than 65,000,000 fathers.

CHAPTER 12

THE POWER OF HOPE

For I know the thoughts that I think toward you, says the Lord,
thoughts of peace and not of evil, to give you a future
and a hope. Then you will call upon Me and go
and pray to Me, and I will listen to you.

—

JEREMIAH 29:11-12 NKJV

Are you a hope-filled pop? You should be. After all, God is good; His love endures; and He has offered you the priceless gift of eternal life. But sometimes hope slips away, even for the most optimistic Christians. Despite God's promises, despite Christ's love, and despite our countless blessings, we can still fall prey to discouragement and doubt. When we do, we need the encouragement of fellow believers, the life-changing power of prayer, and the healing truth of God's Holy Word.

If you find yourself falling into the spiritual traps of worry and discouragement, seek the healing touch of Jesus and the encouraging words of fellow Christians. This world can be a place of trials and tribulations, but as believers, we are secure. God has promised us peace, joy, and eternal life. And, of course, God keeps His promises today, tomorrow, and forever.

MORE GREAT IDEAS ABOUT
HOPE

Our hope in Christ for the future is the mainstream of our joy.

C. H. SPURGEON

Oh, remember this: There is never a time when we may not hope in God. Whatever our necessities, however great our difficulties, and though to all appearance help is impossible, yet our business is to hope in God, and it will be found that it is not in vain.

GEORGE MUELLER

Faith looks back and draws courage; hope looks ahead and keeps desire alive.

JOHN ELDREDGE

Hope is nothing more than the expectation of those things which faith has believed to be truly promised by God.

JOHN CALVIN

Troubles we bear trustfully can bring us a fresh vision of God and a new outlook on life, an outlook of peace and hope.

BILLY GRAHAM

People are genuinely motivated by hope and a part of that hope is the assurance of future glory with God for those who are His people.

WARREN WIERSBE

Never yield to gloomy anticipation. Place your hope and confidence in God. He has no record of failure.

MRS. CHARLES E. COWMAN

The hope we have in Jesus is the anchor for the soul— something sure and steadfast, preventing drifting or giving way, lowered to the depth of God's love.

FRANKLIN GRAHAM

When you accept the fact that sometimes seasons are dry and times are hard and that God is in control of both, you will discover a sense of divine refuge because the hope then is in God and not in yourself.

CHARLES SWINDOLL

MORE WISDOM FROM GOD'S WORD

But if we hope for what we do not see, we eagerly wait for it with patience.

ROMANS 8:25 HCSB

Now may the God of hope fill you with all joy and peace in believing, so that you may overflow with hope by the power of the Holy Spirit.

ROMANS 15:13 HCSB

Rejoice in hope; be patient in affliction; be persistent in prayer.

ROMANS 12:12 HCSB

Lord, I turn my hope to You. My God, I trust in You. Do not let me be disgraced; do not let my enemies gloat over me.

PSALM 25:1-2 HCSB

Let us hold on to the confession of our hope without wavering, for He who promised is faithful.

HEBREWS 10:23 HCSB

TRUST GOD

Sometimes the future seems bright, and sometimes it does not. Yet even when we cannot see the possibilities of tomorrow, God can. As believers, our challenge is to trust an uncertain future to an all-powerful God.

When we trust God, we should trust Him without reservation. We should steel ourselves against the inevitable disappointments of the day, secure in the knowledge that our Heavenly Father has a plan for the future that only He can see.

Can you place your future into the hands of a loving and all-knowing God? Can you live amid the uncertainties of today, knowing that God has dominion over all your tomorrows? If you can, you are wise and you are blessed. When you trust God with everything you are and everything you have, He will bless you now and forever.

MORE GOOD IDEAS

Trusting in my own mental understanding becomes a hindrance to complete trust in God.

OSWALD CHAMBERS

God has proven himself as a faithful father. Now it falls to us to be trusting children.

MAX LUCADO

Never be afraid to trust an unknown future to a known God.

CORRIE TEN BOOM

A TIMELY TIP

If you're experiencing hard times, you'll be wise to start spending more time with God. And if you do your part, God will do His part. So never be afraid to hope—or to ask—for a miracle.

DEAR DAD,
On the Lines Below, Write Down Your Own Ideas About
The Need for Hope

_____

_____

_____

_____

_____

_____

_____

_____

_____

_____

_____

_____

_____

_____

_____

_____

_____

_____

_____

_____

_____

AND FINALLY . . .

WHEN THINGS SEEM HOPELESS,
KEEP HOPING AND GET HOPPING.

CHAPTER 13

FATHERS WHO LIVE IN TRUTH

For everyone who practices wicked things hates the light
and avoids it, so that his deeds may not be exposed.
But anyone who lives by the truth comes to the light,
so that his works may be shown to be accomplished by God.

—

JOHN 3:20–21 HCSB

I t has been said on many occasions and in many ways that honesty is the best policy. For believers, it is far more important to note that honesty is God's policy. And if we are to be servants worthy of Jesus Christ, we must be honest and forthright in our communications with others. Sometimes, honesty is difficult; sometimes, honesty is painful; sometimes, honesty is inconvenient; but always honesty is God's commandment.

In the Book of Proverbs, we read, "The Lord detests lying lips, but he delights in men who are truthful" (12:22 NIV). Clearly, we must strive to be men whose words are pleasing to our Creator. Truth is God's way, and it must be our way, too, even when telling the truth is difficult. As loving fathers, we can do no less.

MORE GREAT IDEAS ABOUT
TRUTH

You cannot glorify Christ and practice deception at the same time.

WARREN WIERSBE

Honesty has a beautiful and refreshing simplicity about it. No ulterior motives. No hidden meanings. As honesty and integrity characterize our lives, there will be no need to manipulate others.

CHARLES SWINDOLL

Lying covers a multitude of sins—temporarily.

D. L. MOODY

The only people who achieve much are those who want knowledge so badly that they seek it while the conditions are still unfavorable. Favorable conditions never come.

C. S. LEWIS

For Christians, God himself is the only absolute; truth and ethics are rooted in his character.

CHUCK COLSON

We have in Jesus Christ a perfect example of how to put God's truth into practice.

BILL BRIGHT

Truth will triumph. The Father of truth will win, and the followers of truth will be saved.

MAX LUCADO

Having a doctrine pass before the mind is not what the Bible means by knowing the truth. It's only when it reaches down deep into the heart that the truth begins to set us free, just as a key must penetrate a lock to turn it or as rainfall must saturate the earth down to the roots in order for your garden to grow.

JOHN ELDREDGE

To worship Him in truth means to worship Him honestly, without hypocrisy, standing open and transparent before Him.

ANNE GRAHAM LOTZ

God will see to it that we understand as much truth as we are willing to obey.

ELISABETH ELLIOT

MORE WISDOM FROM GOD'S WORD

Be diligent to present yourself approved to God, a worker who doesn't need to be ashamed, correctly teaching the word of truth.

2 TIMOTHY 2:15 HCSB

I have no greater joy than this: to hear that my children are walking in the truth.

3 JOHN 1:4 HCSB

You have already heard about this hope in the message of truth, the gospel that has come to you. It is bearing fruit and growing all over the world, just as it has among you since the day you heard it and recognized God's grace in the truth.

COLOSSIANS 1:5-6 HCSB

When the Spirit of truth comes, He will guide you into all the truth.

JOHN 16:13 HCSB

The entirety of Your word is truth, and all Your righteous judgments endure forever.

PSALM 119:160 HCSB

MORE GOOD IDEAS

Only Jesus Christ is the truth for everyone who has ever been born into the human race, regardless of culture, age, nationality, generation, heritage, gender, color, or language.

ANNE GRAHAM LOTZ

Those who walk in truth walk in liberty.

BETH MOORE

Having truth decay? Brush up on your Bible!

ANONYMOUS

A TIMELY TIP

Warren Wiersbe writes, "Learning God's truth and getting it into our heads is one thing, but living God's truth and getting it into our characters is quite something else." So don't be satisfied to sit on the sidelines and observe the truth at a distance—live it.

DEAR DAD,
On the Lines Below, Write Down Your Own Ideas About
Truth

CHAPTER 14

THE IMPORTANCE OF WORSHIP

But an hour is coming, and is now here, when the true
worshipers will worship the Father in spirit and truth.
Yes, the Father wants such people to worship Him.
God is Spirit, and those who worship Him
must worship in spirit and truth.

—

JOHN 4:23-24 HCSB

When you lead your family in worship, you are to be praised. By worshipping your Creator—and by teaching your children to do likewise—you make a powerful statement about the place that God occupies in your life.

Ours is a society in which too many men have abandoned the moral leadership of their families, often with tragic consequences. Men who neglect to worship God, either thoughtlessly or intentionally, invite untold suffering into their own lives and into the lives of their loved ones.

Every day provides opportunities to put God where He belongs: at the center of our hearts. May we worship Him, and only Him, always. And, may we encourage the members of our family to do the same.

MORE GREAT IDEAS ABOUT WORSHIP

I am of the opinion that we should not be concerned about working for God until we have learned the meaning and delight of worshipping Him.

A. W. TOZER

When God is at the center of your life, you worship. When he's not, you worry.

RICK WARREN

Each time, before you intercede, be quiet first and worship God in His glory. Think of what He can do and how He delights to hear the prayers of His redeemed people. Think of your place and privilege in Christ, and expect great things!

ANDREW MURRAY

Worship is spiritual. Our worship must be more than just outward expression; it must also take place in our spirits.

FRANKLIN GRAHAM

Inside the human heart is an undeniable, spiritual instinct to commune with its Creator.

JIM CYMBALA

Worship is a daunting task. Each worships differently. But each should worship.

MAX LUCADO

The New Testament does not envisage solitary religion; some kind of regular assembly for worship and instruction is everywhere taken for granted in the Epistles.

C. S. LEWIS

Worship is your spirit responding to God's Spirit.

RICK WARREN

Spiritual worship comes from our very core and is fueled by an awesome reverence and desire for God.

BETH MOORE

Worship is not taught from the pulpit. It must be learned in the heart.

JIM ELLIOT

MORE WISDOM FROM GOD'S WORD

So that at the name of Jesus every knee should bow—of those who are in heaven and on earth and under the earth—and every tongue should confess that Jesus Christ is Lord, to the glory of God the Father.

PHILIPPIANS 2:10-11 HCSB

Worship the Lord your God and . . . serve Him only.

MATTHEW 4:10 HCSB

If anyone is thirsty, he should come to Me and drink!

JOHN 7:37 HCSB

And every day they devoted themselves to meeting together in the temple complex, and broke bread from house to house. They ate their food with gladness and simplicity of heart, praising God and having favor with all the people. And every day the Lord added those being saved to them.

ACTS 2:46-47 HCSB

All the earth will worship You and sing praise to You. They will sing praise to Your name.

PSALM 66:4 HCSB

MORE GOOD IDEAS

Worship is an act which develops feelings for God, not a feeling for God which is expressed in an act of worship. When we obey the command to praise God in worship, our deep, essential need to be in relationship with God is nurtured.

EUGENE PETERSON

Another thing I liked about my dad at church: he did his sleeping at home. He never used the church for an adult nursery.

VANCE HAVNER

A TIMELY TIP

Worship reminds you of the awesome power of God. So worship Him daily, and allow Him to work through you every day of the week (not just on Sunday).

DEAR DAD,
On the Lines Below, Write Down Your Own Ideas About
The Importance of Worship

_____

_____

_____

_____

_____

_____

_____

_____

_____

_____

_____

_____

_____

_____

_____

_____

_____

_____

_____

_____

_____

CHAPTER 15

FINDING PEACE

The peace of God, which surpasses all understanding,
will guard your hearts and minds through Christ Jesus.

—

PHILIPPIANS 4:7 NKJV

As a busy father, your plate is probably full: kids to care for, bills to pay, a family to lead. Sometimes it seems that you can scarcely find a moment's peace. But the beautiful words of John 14:27 are a reminder that God's peace is always available to you.

Jesus said, "Peace I leave with you, my peace I give unto you . . . ." Christ offers us peace, not as the world gives, but as He alone gives. We, as believers, can accept His peace or ignore it.

When we accept the peace of Jesus Christ into our hearts, our lives are transformed. And then, because we possess the gift of peace, we can share that gift with fellow Christians, family members, friends, and associates. If, on the other hand, we choose to ignore the gift of peace—for whatever reason—we simply cannot share what we do not possess.

Today, as a gift to yourself, to your family, and to your friends, claim the inner peace that is your spiritual birthright: the peace of Jesus Christ. It is offered freely; it has been paid for in full; it is yours for the asking. So ask. And then share.

MORE GREAT IDEAS ABOUT
PEACE

We're prone to want God to change our circumstances, but He wants to change our character. We think that peace comes from the outside in, but it comes from the inside out.

WARREN WIERSBE

Thou hast formed us for Thyself, and our hearts are restless till they find rest in Thee.

ST. AUGUSTINE

Peace is the deepest thing a human personality can know; it is almighty.

OSWALD CHAMBERS

What peace can they have who are not at peace with God?

MATTHEW HENRY

That peace, which has been described and which believers enjoy, is a participation of the peace which their glorious Lord and Master himself enjoys.

JONATHAN EDWARDS

A great many people are trying to make peace, but that has already been done. God has not left it for us to do; all we have to do is to enter into it.

D. L. MOODY

He keeps us in perfect peace while He whispers His secrets and reveals His counsels.

OSWALD CHAMBERS

Peace with God is where all peace begins.

JIM GALLERY

When we do what is right, we have contentment, peace, and happiness.

BEVERLY LaHAYE

To know God as He really is—in His essential nature and character—is to arrive at a citadel of peace that circumstances may storm, but can never capture.

CATHERINE MARSHALL

MORE WISDOM FROM GOD'S WORD

If possible, on your part, live at peace with everyone.

ROMANS 12:18 HCSB

Abundant peace belongs to those who love Your instruction; nothing makes them stumble.

PSALM 119:165 HCSB

Blessed are the peacemakers, for they shall be called sons of God.

MATTHEW 5:9 NKJV

And suddenly there was with the angel a multitude of the heavenly host praising God and saying: "Glory to God in the highest, And on earth peace, goodwill toward men!"

LUKE 2:13-14 NKJV

So then, we must pursue what promotes peace and what builds up one another.

ROMANS 14:19 HCSB

FINDING PEACE IN THE STORM

A frightening storm rose quickly on the Sea of Galilee, and the disciples were afraid. Because of their limited faith, they feared for their lives. When they turned to Jesus, He calmed the waters and He rebuked His disciples for their lack of faith in Him.

On occasion, we, like the disciples, are frightened by the inevitable storms of life. Why are we afraid? Because we, like the disciples, possess imperfect faith.

When we genuinely accept God's promises as absolute truth, when we trust Him with life here on earth and life eternal, we have little to fear. Faith in God is the antidote to worry. Faith in God is the foundation of courage and the source of power. Today, let us trust God more completely and, by doing so, move beyond our fears to a place of abundance, assurance, and peace.

MORE GOOD IDEAS

In the center of a hurricane there is absolute quiet and peace. There is no safer place than in the center of the will of God.

CORRIE TEN BOOM

For Jesus peace seems to have meant not the absence of struggle but the presence of love.

FREDERICK BUECHNER

The fruit of our placing all things in God's hands is the presence of His abiding peace in our hearts.

HANNAH WHITALL SMITH

A TIMELY TIP

Do you want to discover God's peace? Then do your best to live in the center of God's will.

DEAR DAD,
On the Lines Below, Write Down Your Own Ideas About Ways to Live a More Peaceful Life

AND FINALLY . . .

Keep your family from the abominable practice
of backbiting.

—

THE OLD FARMER'S ALMANAC, 1811

CHAPTER 16

THE POWER OF COURAGE

The Lord is the One who will go before you.
He will be with you; He will not leave you or forsake you.
Do not be afraid or discouraged.

—

DEUTERONOMY 31:8 HCSB

Being a godly father in this difficult world is no easy task. Ours is a time of uncertainty and danger, a time when even the most courageous dads have legitimate cause for concern. But as believers we can live courageously, knowing that we have been saved by a loving Father and His only begotten Son.

Are you anxious? Take those anxieties to God. Are you troubled? Take your troubles to Him. Does the world seem to be trembling beneath your feet? Seek protection from the One who cannot be moved. The same God who created the universe will protect you if you ask Him . . . so ask Him. And then live courageously, knowing that even in these troubled times, God is always as near as your next breath.

MORE GREAT IDEAS ABOUT
COURAGE

Down through the centuries, in times of trouble and trial, God has brought courage to the hearts of those who love Him. The Bible is filled with assurances of God's help and comfort in every kind of trouble which might cause fears to arise in the human heart. You can look ahead with promise, hope, and joy.

BILLY GRAHAM

Jesus Christ can make the weakest man into a divine dreadnought, fearing nothing.

OSWALD CHAMBERS

There comes a time when we simply have to face the challenges in our lives and stop backing down.

JOHN ELDREDGE

Faith not only can help you through a crisis, it can help you to approach life after the hard times with a whole new perspective. It can help you adopt an outlook of hope and courage through faith to face reality.

JOHN MAXWELL

Take courage. We walk in the wilderness today and in the Promised Land tomorrow.

D. L. MOODY

Why rely on yourself and fall? Cast yourself upon His arm. Be not afraid. He will not let you slip. Cast yourself in confidence. He will receive you and heal you.

ST. AUGUSTINE

Do not let Satan deceive you into being afraid of God's plans for your life.

R. A. TORREY

Are you fearful? First, bow your head and pray for God's strength. Then, raise your head knowing that, together, you and God can handle whatever comes your way.

JIM GALLERY

If a person fears God, he or she has no reason to fear anything else. On the other hand, if a person does not fear God, then fear becomes a way of life.

BETH MOORE

MORE WISDOM FROM GOD'S WORD

For God has not given us a spirit of fearfulness, but one of power, love, and sound judgment.

2 TIMOTHY 1:7 HCSB

Be alert, stand firm in the faith, be brave and strong.

1 CORINTHIANS 16:13 HCSB

Haven't I commanded you: be strong and courageous? Do not be afraid or discouraged, for the Lord your God is with you wherever you go.

JOSHUA 1:9 HCSB

But when Jesus heard it, He answered him, "Don't be afraid. Only believe."

LUKE 8:50 HCSB

So we may boldly say: "The Lord is my helper; I will not fear. What can man do to me?"

HEBREWS 13:6 NKJV

IF

If you can keep your head when all about you
Are losing theirs and blaming it on you;
If you can trust yourself when all men doubt you
But make allowance for their doubting too;
If you can wait and not be tired by waiting,
Or, being lied about, don't deal in lies,
Or, being hated, don't give way to hating,
And yet don't look too good, nor talk too wise;

If you can dream—and not make dreams your master;
If you can think—and not make thoughts your aim;
If you can meet with triumph and disaster
And treat those two imposters just the same;
If you can bear to hear the truth you've spoken
Twisted by knaves to make a trap for fools,
Or watch the things you gave your life to, broken
And stoop and build 'em up with worn-out tools;

If you can make one heap of all your winnings
And risk it on one turn of pitch-and-toss,
And lose, and start again at your beginnings
And never breathe a word about your loss;
If you can force your heart and nerve and sinew
To serve your turn long after they are gone,
And so hold on when there is nothing in you
Except the Will which says to them: "Hold on!";

If you can talk with crowds and keep your virtue,
Or walk with kings—nor lose the common touch;
If neither foes nor loving friends can hurt you;
If all men count with you, but none too much;
If you can fill the unforgiving minute
With sixty seconds' worth of distance run—
Yours is the Earth and everything that's in it,
And—which is more—you'll be a Man, my son!

RUDYARD KIPLING

A TIMELY TIP

Courage is contagious, and courage inspired by a steadfast trust in a loving Heavenly Father is highly contagious. Today, as you interact with friends, family members, or co-workers, share your courage, your hopes, your dreams, and your enthusiasm. Your positive outlook will be almost as big a blessing to them as it is to you.

DEAR DAD,
On the Lines Below, Write Down Your Own Ideas About
The Rewards of Living Courageously

AND FINALLY . . .

DID YOU KNOW?

In 1924, President Calvin Coolidge made Father's Day a national event.

CHAPTER 17

FATHERS WHO OBEY GOD

Therefore, get your minds ready for action,
being self-disciplined, and set your hope completely on
the grace to be brought to you at the revelation of Jesus Christ.
As obedient children, do not be conformed to the desires
of your former ignorance but, as the One who called you
is holy, you also are to be holy in all your conduct.

—

1 PETER 1:13-15 HCSB

We live in a world filled with temptations, distractions, and countless opportunities to disobey God. But as men who seek to be godly role models for our families, we must turn our thoughts and our hearts away from the evils of this world. We must turn instead to God.

Talking about God is easy; living by His commandments is considerably harder. But unless we are willing to abide by God's laws, our righteous proclamations ring hollow.

How can we best proclaim our love for the Lord? By obeying Him. We must seek God's counsel and trust the counsel He gives. And, when we invite God into our hearts and live according to His commandments, we are blessed today and tomorrow and forever.

MORE GREAT IDEAS ABOUT
OBEDIENCE

Mary could not have dreamed all that would result from her faithful obedience. Likewise, you cannot possibly imagine all that God has in store for you when you trust him.

HENRY BLACKABY

Only he who believes is obedient. Only he who is obedient believes.

DIETRICH BONHOEFFER

When you suffer and lose, that does not mean you are being disobedient to God. In fact, it might mean you're right in the center of His will. The path of obedience is often marked by times of suffering and loss.

CHARLES SWINDOLL

You can't step in front of God and not get in trouble. When He says, "Go three steps," don't go four.

CHARLES STANLEY

Trials and sufferings teach us to obey the Lord by faith, and we soon learn that obedience pays off in joyful ways.

BILL BRIGHT

Obedience is the road to freedom, humility the road to pleasure, unity the road to personality.

C. S. LEWIS

Let your fellowship with the Father and with the Lord Jesus Christ have as its one aim and object a life of quiet, determined, unquestioning obedience.

ANDREW MURRAY

You may not always see immediate results, but all God wants is your obedience and faithfulness.

VONETTE BRIGHT

I don't always like His decisions, but when I choose to obey Him, the act of obedience still "counts" with Him even if I'm not thrilled about it.

BETH MOORE

True faith commits us to obedience.

A. W. TOZER

MORE WISDOM FROM GOD'S WORD

I have sought You with all my heart; don't let me wander from Your commands.

PSALM 119:10 HCSB

Therefore, everyone who hears these words of Mine and acts on them will be like a sensible man who built his house on the rock. The rain fell, the rivers rose, and the winds blew and pounded that house. Yet it didn't collapse, because its foundation was on the rock.

MATTHEW 7:24–25 HCSB

Just then someone came up and asked Him, "Teacher, what good must I do to have eternal life?" "Why do you ask Me about what is good?" He said to him. "There is only One who is good. If you want to enter into life, keep the commandments."

MATTHEW 19:16-17 HCSB

Jesus answered, "If anyone loves Me, he will keep My word. My Father will love him, and We will come to him and make Our home with him."

JOHN 14:23 HCSB

DOING WHAT'S RIGHT

Life is a series of choices. Each day, we make countless decisions that can bring us closer to God . . . or not. When we live according to God's commandments, we earn for ourselves the abundance and peace that He intends for our lives. But, when we turn our backs upon God by disobeying Him, we bring needless suffering upon ourselves and our families.

Do you seek God's peace and His blessings? Then obey Him. When you're faced with a difficult choice or a powerful temptation, seek God's counsel and trust the counsel He gives. Invite God into your heart and live according to His commandments. When you do, you will be blessed today and tomorrow and forever.

MORE GOOD IDEAS

Every day, I find countless opportunities to decide whether I will obey God and demonstrate my love for Him or try to please myself or the world system. God is waiting for my choices.

BILL BRIGHT

Every time you make a choice, you are turning the central part of you, the part that chooses, into something a little different from what it was before.

C. S. LEWIS

God always gives His best to those who leave the choice with Him.

JIM ELLIOT

A TIMELY TIP

Your children will learn about life from many sources; the most important source should be you. But remember that the lectures you give are never as important as the ones you live.

DEAR DAD,

On the Lines Below, Write Down Your Own Ideas About The Rewards of Doing the Right Thing

AND FINALLY . . .

A FATHER IS A MAN WHO
CAN'T GET ON THE PHONE,
INTO THE BATHROOM,
OR OUT OF THE HOUSE.

CHAPTER 18

LIFETIME LEARNING

*Now if any of you lacks wisdom, he should ask God,
who gives to all generously and without criticizing,
and it will be given to him.*

—

JAMES 1:5 HCSB

Whether you're twenty-two or a hundred and two, you've still got lots to learn. Even if you're a very wise man, God isn't finished with you yet, and He isn't finished teaching you important lessons about life here on earth and life eternal.

Do you seek to live a life of righteousness and wisdom? If so, you must continue to study the ultimate source of wisdom: the Word of God. You must associate, day in and day out, with godly men and women. And, you must act in accordance with your beliefs. When you study God's Word and live according to His commandments, you will become wise . . . and you will be a blessing to your friends, to your family, and to the world.

MORE GREAT IDEAS ABOUT
LIFETIME LEARNING

Kids aren't looking for perfect parents, but they are looking for honest and growing ones.

HOWARD HENDRICKS

Don't expect wisdom to come into your life like great chunks of rock on a conveyor belt. Wisdom comes privately from God as a by-product of right decisions, godly reactions, and the application of spiritual principles to daily circumstances.

CHARLES SWINDOLL

Wise people listen to wise instruction, especially instruction from the Word of God.

WARREN WIERSBE

It's the things you learn after you know it all that really count.

VANCE HAVNER

We often become mentally and spiritually barren because we're so busy.

FRANKLIN GRAHAM

The vigor of our spiritual lives will be in exact proportion to the place held by the Bible in our lives and in our thoughts.

GEORGE MUELLER

God's plan for our guidance is for us to grow gradually in wisdom before we get to the crossroads.

BILL HYBELS

The wise man gives proper appreciation in his life to his past. He learns to sift the sawdust of heritage in order to find the nuggets that make the current moment have any meaning.

GRADY NUTT

He who is ashamed of asking is ashamed of learning.

OLD SAYING

MORE WISDOM FROM GOD'S WORD

Buy—and do not sell—truth, wisdom, instruction, and understanding.

PROVERBS 23:23 HCSB

For this very reason, make every effort to supplement your faith with goodness, goodness with knowledge, knowledge with self-control, self-control with endurance, endurance with godliness.

2 PETER 1:5-6 HCSB

Wisdom is the principal thing; therefore get wisdom. And in all your getting, get understanding.

PROVERBS 4:7 NKJV

For now we see indistinctly, as in a mirror, but then face to face. Now I know in part, but then I will know fully, as I am fully known.

1 CORINTHIANS 13:12 HCSB

An ear that listens to life-giving rebukes will be at home among the wise.

PROVERBS 15:31 HCSB

MORE GOOD IDEAS

Learn from everyone.

BEN FRANKLIN

Those things that hurt, instruct.

BEN FRANKLIN

Being ignorant is not so much a shame as being unwilling to learn.

BEN FRANKLIN

A TIMELY TIP

God still has important lessons to teach you. Your task is to be open to His instruction.

DEAR DAD,
On the Lines Below, Write Down Your Own Ideas About Lifetime Learning

_____

_____

_____

_____

_____

_____

_____

_____

_____

_____

_____

_____

_____

_____

_____

_____

_____

_____

_____

_____

_____

_____

CHAPTER 19

FORGIVENESS NOW

*All bitterness, anger and wrath, insult and slander
must be removed from you, along with all wickedness.
And be kind and compassionate to one another,
forgiving one another, just as God also forgave you in Christ.*

—

EPHESIANS 4:31-32 HCSB

Even the most mild-mannered dads will, on occasion, have reason to become angry with the shortcomings of family members and friends. But wise dads are quick to forgive others, just as God has forgiven them.

Forgiveness is God's commandment, but oh how difficult a commandment it can be to follow. Being frail, fallible, imperfect human beings, we are quick to anger, quick to blame, slow to forgive, and even slower to forget. No matter. Forgiveness, no matter how difficult, is God's way, and it must be our way, too.

If, in your heart, you hold bitterness against even a single person, forgive. If there exists even one person, alive or dead, whom you have not forgiven, follow God's commandment and His will for your life: forgive. If you are embittered against yourself for some past mistake or shortcoming, forgive. Then, to the best of your abilities, forget. And move on. Hatred and bitterness and regret are not part of God's plan for your life. Forgiveness is.

MORE GREAT IDEAS ABOUT FORGIVENESS

Give me such love for God and men as will blot out all hatred and bitterness.

DIETRICH BONHOEFFER

God forgets the past. Imitate him.

MAX LUCADO

To hold on to hate and resentments is to throw a monkey wrench into the machinery of life.

E. STANLEY JONES

Our forgiveness toward others should flow from a realization and appreciation of God's forgiveness toward us.

FRANKLIN GRAHAM

By not forgiving, by not letting wrongs go, we aren't getting back at anyone. We are merely punishing ourselves by barricading our own hearts.

JIM CYMBALA

Forgiveness is God's command.

MARTIN LUTHER

The love of God is revealed in that He laid down His life for His enemies.

OSWALD CHAMBERS

Forgiveness is the key that unlocks the door of resentment and the handcuffs of hate. It is a power that breaks the chains of bitterness and the shackles of selfishness.

CORRIE TEN BOOM

Miracles broke the physical laws of the universe; forgiveness broke the moral rules.

PHILIP YANCEY

If you're going to forgive somebody eventually, why wait?

MARIE T. FREEMAN

MORE WISDOM FROM GOD'S WORD

See to it that no one repays evil for evil to anyone, but always pursue what is good for one another and for all.

1 THESSALONIANS 5:15 HCSB

A person's insight gives him patience, and his virtue is to overlook an offense.

PROVERBS 19:11 HCSB

And forgive us our sins, for we ourselves also forgive everyone in debt to us.

LUKE 11:4 HCSB

Be merciful, just as your Father also is merciful.

LUKE 6:36 HCSB

When they persisted in questioning Him, He stood up and said to them, "The one without sin among you should be the first to throw a stone at her."

JOHN 8:7 HCSB

BEYOND REGRET

Have you made peace with your past? If so, congratulations. But, if you are mired in the quicksand of regret, it's time to plan your escape. How can you do so? By accepting what has been and by trusting God for what will be.

Because you are human, you may be slow to forget yesterday's disappointments; if so you are not alone. But if you sincerely seek to focus your hopes and energies on the future, then you must find ways to accept the past, no matter how difficult it may be to do so.

If you have not yet made peace with the past, today is the day to declare an end to all hostilities. When you do, you can then turn your thoughts to the wondrous promises of God and to the glorious future that He has in store for you.

MORE GOOD IDEAS

Reflect upon your present blessings, of which every man has many—not on your past misfortunes, of which all men have some.

CHARLES DICKENS

Regret is an appalling waste of energy; you can't build on it; it is good only for wallowing.

KATHERINE MANSFIELD

To be happy, drop the words "if only," and substitute instead the words "next time."

SMILEY BLANTON

A TIMELY TIP

If forgiveness were easy, everybody would be doing it. But of course forgiveness can, at times, be a very hard thing to do. So be quick to explain to your child that forgiving another person—even when it's difficult—is the correct thing to do.

DEAR DAD,
On the Lines Below, Write Down Your Own Ideas About The Need to Forgive

AND FINALLY . . .

WHEN YOU HARBOR BITTERNESS,
HAPPINESS WILL DOCK ELSEWHERE.

CHAPTER 20

FATHERS WHO ARE FAITHFUL STEWARDS

*Let a man so consider us, as servants of Christ
and stewards of the mysteries of God.
Moreover it is required in stewards that one be found faithful.*

—

1 CORINTHIANS 4:1-2 NKJV

How will you serve God? Will you give Him the firstfruits of your harvest? Will you honor Him with the best you have to offer? Will you praise the Creator not only with your words but also with your deeds?

Every day is a fresh opportunity to honor God with your prayers, with your praise, with your deeds, and with your testimony. Your Heavenly Father deserves no less.

Does the level of your stewardship honor the One who has given you everything? If so, God will bless you because of your obedience. And if your stewardship has been somehow deficient, the best day to begin serving Him more faithfully is today.

MORE GREAT IDEAS ABOUT
STEWARDSHIP

A steward does not own, but instead manages, all that his master puts into his hands.

WARREN WIERSBE

Selfishness is as far from Christianity as darkness is from light.

C. H. SPURGEON

Christians have become victims of one of the most devious plots Satan ever created—the concept that money belongs to us and not to God.

LARRY BURKETT

If our charities do not at all pinch or hamper us, I should say they are too small. There ought to be things we should like to do and cannot do because our charitable expenditure excludes them.

C. S. LEWIS

We are never more like God than when we give.

CHARLES SWINDOLL

God will withdraw resources from the poor stewards, as related in Matthew 25, and give it to the good stewards.

BILL BRIGHT

A steward is one who manages another's resources. Each of us is a manager, not an owner. God is the owner, and we are to manage according to His plan.

LARRY BURKETT

You can sing your heart out but never give back to God, and you'll miss the fullness of worship.

DAVE RAMSEY

The mark of a Christian is that he will walk the second mile and turn the other cheek. A wise man or woman gives the extra effort, all for the glory of the Lord Jesus Christ.

JOHN MAXWELL

As faithful stewards of what we have, ought we not to give earnest thought to our staggering surplus?

ELISABETH ELLIOT

MORE WISDOM FROM GOD'S WORD

Based on the gift they have received, everyone should use it to serve others, as good managers of the varied grace of God.

1 PETER 4:10 HCSB

Well done, good and faithful servant; you were faithful over a few things, I will make you ruler over many things. Enter into the joy of your lord.

MATTHEW 25:21 NKJV

He that giveth, let him do it with simplicity . . . .

ROMANS 12:8 KJV

Every tenth of the land's produce, grain from the soil or fruit from the trees, belongs to the Lord; it is holy to the Lord.

LEVITICUS 27:30 HCSB

For I am the Lord, I do not change. Will a man rob God? Yet you have robbed Me! But you say, in what way have we robbed You? In tithes and offerings. You are cursed with a curse, for you have robbed Me, even this whole nation. Bring all the tithes into the storehouse, that there may be food in My house.

MALACHI 3:6,8-10 NKJV

MORE GOOD IDEAS

If you desire to become a more generous person, don't wait for your income to change. Change your heart.

JOHN MAXWELL

If we can learn to develop a giving heart toward those in our own homes and families, we'll be much more free to give ungrudgingly—and at the Spirit's prompting—to those in the most desperate need.

MARY HUNT

The measure of a life, after all, is not its duration but its donation.

CORRIE TEN BOOM

A TIMELY TIP

A good steward knows that . . . everything comes from God, and everything God has is available to those who are good stewards.

DEAR DAD,
On the Lines Below, Write Down Your Own Ideas About Stewardship

_____

_____

_____

_____

_____

_____

_____

_____

_____

_____

_____

_____

_____

_____

_____

_____

_____

_____

_____

CHAPTER 21

FATHERS WHO LIVE HUMBLY

Do nothing out of rivalry or conceit, but in humility consider others as more important than yourselves.

—

PHILIPPIANS 2:3 HCSB

Hopefully, you are a proud papa. God intends that you take appropriate parental pride in every member of your family. But God has a stern warning for those who would take undo pride in their own accomplishments. Excessive pride is a sin.

As Christians, we have a profound reason to be humble: We have been refashioned and saved by Jesus Christ, and that salvation came not because of our own good works but because of God's grace. Thus, we are not "self-made"; we are "God-made" and "Christ-saved." How, then, can we be boastful? The answer, of course, is simple: if we are to be honest with ourselves and with our God, we cannot be boastful. In the quiet moments, when we search the depths of our own hearts, we know that whatever "it" is, God did that. And He deserves the credit.

MORE GREAT IDEAS ABOUT
HUMILITY

We can never have more of true faith than we have of true humility.

ANDREW MURRAY

Jesus had a humble heart. If He abides in us, pride will never dominate our lives.

BILLY GRAHAM

Humility is the fairest and rarest flower that blooms.

CHARLES SWINDOLL

Humility is an attitude. The Lord is high and lifted up, and we are supposed to take a position of lowliness.

FRANKLIN GRAHAM

Let the love of Christ be believed in and felt in your hearts, and it will humble you.

C. H. SPURGEON

A humble heart is like a magnet that draws the favor of God toward us.

JIM CYMBALA

Nothing sets a person so much out of the devil's reach as humility.

JONATHAN EDWARDS

It is one of the most beautiful compensations of life that no one can sincerely try to help another without helping herself.

BARBARA JOHNSON

Kindness in this world will do much to help others, not only to come into the light, but also to grow in grace day by day.

FANNY CROSBY

Because Christ Jesus came to the world clothed in humility, he will always be found among those who are clothed with humility. He will be found among the humble people.

A. W. TOZER

MORE WISDOM FROM GOD'S WORD

Humble yourselves therefore under the mighty hand of God, so that He may exalt you in due time, casting all your care upon Him, because He cares about you.

1 PETER 5:6-7 HCSB

But He said to me, "My grace is sufficient for you, for power is perfected in weakness." Therefore, I will most gladly boast all the more about my weaknesses, so that Christ's power may reside in me.

2 CORINTHIANS 12:9 HCSB

You will save the humble people; but Your eyes are on the haughty, that You may bring them down.

2 SAMUEL 22:28 NKJV

If My people who are called by My name will humble themselves, and pray and seek My face, and turn from their wicked ways, then I will hear from heaven, and will forgive their sin and heal their land.

2 CHRONICLES 7:14 NKJV

Humble yourselves before the Lord, and He will exalt you.

JAMES 4:10 HCSB

MORE GOOD IDEAS

Life is a long lesson in humility.

JAMES BARRIE

Don't talk too much or too soon.

BEAR BRYANT

A man wrapped up in himself makes a very small package.

BEN FRANKLIN

A TIMELY TIP

Remember that humility leads to happiness, and pride doesn't. Max Lucado writes, "God exalts humility. When God works in our lives, helping us to become humble, he gives us a permanent joy. Humility gives us a joy that cannot be taken away." Enough said.

DEAR DAD,
On the Lines Below, Write Down Your Own Ideas About Humility

_____

_____

_____

_____

_____

_____

_____

_____

_____

_____

_____

_____

_____

_____

_____

_____

_____

_____

_____

_____

_____

CHAPTER 22

FATHERS WHO OBEY THE GOLDEN RULE

*Just as you want others to do for you,
do the same for them.*

—

LUKE 6:31 HCSB

The words of Matthew 7:12 remind us that, as believers in Christ, we are commanded to treat others as we wish to be treated. This commandment is, indeed, the Golden Rule for Christians of every generation. When we weave the thread of kindness into the very fabric of our lives, we give glory to the One who gave His life for ours.

Because we are imperfect human beings, we are, on occasion, selfish, thoughtless, or cruel. But God commands us to behave otherwise. He teaches us to rise above our own imperfections and to treat others with unselfishness and love. When we observe God's Golden Rule, we help build His kingdom here on earth. And, when we share the love of Christ, we share a priceless gift; may we share it today and every day that we live.

MORE GREAT IDEAS ABOUT THE GOLDEN RULE

Do all the good you can. By all the means you can. In all the ways you can. In all the places you can. At all the times you can. To all the people you can. As long as you can.

JOHN WESLEY

Abundant living means abundant giving.

E. STANLEY JONES

Faith never asks whether good works are to be done, but has done them before there is time to ask the question, and it is always doing them.

MARTIN LUTHER

Our lives, we are told, are but fleeting at best, / Like roses they fade and decay; / Then let us do good while the present is ours, / Be useful as long as we stay.

FANNY CROSBY

The Golden Rule starts at home, but it should never stop there.

MARIE T. FREEMAN

The #1 rule of friendship is the Golden one.

JIM GALLERY

If you want to be truly happy, you won't find it on an endless quest for more stuff. You'll find it in receiving God's generosity and in passing that generosity along.

BILL HYBELS

We are never more like God than when we give.

CHARLES SWINDOLL

Let no one ever come to you without leaving better and happier. Be the living expression of God's kindness: kindness in your face, kindness in your eyes, kindness in your smile.

MOTHER TERESA

Constant kindness can accomplish much. As the sun makes ice melt, kindness causes misunderstanding, mistrust, and hostility to evaporate.

ALBERT SCHWEITZER

MORE WISDOM FROM GOD'S WORD

If you really carry out the royal law prescribed in Scripture, You shall love your neighbor as yourself, you are doing well.

JAMES 2:8 HCSB

Therefore, whatever you want others to do for you, do also the same for them—this is the Law and the Prophets.

MATTHEW 7:12 HCSB

And let us not grow weary while doing good, for in due season we shall reap if we do not lose heart.

GALATIANS 6:9 NKJV

See that no one renders evil for evil to anyone, but always pursue what is good both for yourselves and for all.

1 THESSALONIANS 5:15 NKJV

Be kindly affectionate to one another with brotherly love, in honor giving preference to one another; not lagging in diligence, fervent in spirit, serving the Lord; rejoicing in hope, patient in tribulation, continuing steadfastly in prayer.

ROMANS 12:10-12 NKJV

BE COURTEOUS

Did Christ instruct us in matters of etiquette and courtesy? Of course He did. Christ's instructions are clear: "In everything, therefore, treat people the same way you want them to treat you, for this is the Law and the Prophets" (Matthew 7:12 NASB). Jesus did not say, "In some things, treat people as you wish to be treated." And, He did not say, "From time to time, treat others with kindness." Christ said that we should treat others as we wish to be treated in every aspect of our daily lives. This, of course, is a tall order indeed, but as Christians, we are commanded to do our best.

Today, promise yourself that you'll do your family (and the world) a king-sized favor by whole-heartedly pursuing your dreams. After all, no dreams are too big for God—not even yours. So start living—and dreaming—accordingly.

More Good Ideas

Reach out and care for someone who needs the touch of hospitality. The time you spend caring today will be a love gift that will blossom into the fresh joy of God's Spirit in the future.

Emilie Barnes

When you extend hospitality to others, you're not trying to impress people; you're trying to reflect God to them.

Max Lucado

Ill customs and bad advice are seldom forgotten.

Ben Franklin

A Timely Tip

When you live according to the principle of the Golden Rule, your children will notice, and the results will be as good as gold . . . make that better than gold!

DEAR DAD,
On the Lines Below, Write Down Your Own Ideas About The Golden Rule

AND FINALLY . . .

DID YOU KNOW?

In 1966 President Lyndon Johnson signed a presidential proclamation declaring the 3rd Sunday of June as Father's Day.

CHAPTER 23

WHEN TIMES ARE TOUGH

Dear friends, when the fiery ordeal arises among you to test you, don't be surprised by it, as if something unusual were happening to you. Instead, as you share in the sufferings of the Messiah rejoice, so that you may also rejoice with great joy at the revelation of His glory.

—

1 PETER 4:12-13 HCSB

Are you a dad who has endured tough times? If so, welcome to the club! From time to time, all of us face adversity, discouragement, or disappointment. When we do, God stands ready to protect us. Psalm 147 promises, "He heals the brokenhearted, and binds their wounds" (v. 3, NIV). When we are troubled, we must call upon God, and then, in His own time and according to His own plan, He will heal us.

Life is often challenging, but as Christians, we must not be afraid. God loves us, and He will protect us. In times of hardship, He will comfort us; in times of sorrow, He will dry our tears. When we are troubled or weak or sorrowful, God is always with us. We must build our lives on the rock that cannot be shaken . . . we must trust in God. Always.

MORE GREAT IDEAS ABOUT ADVERSITY

As sure as God puts his children in the furnace, he will be in the furnace with them.

C. H. SPURGEON

God whispers to us in our pleasures, speaks in our conscience, but shouts in our pain.

C. S. LEWIS

Life will be made or broken at the place where we meet and deal with obstacles.

E. STANLEY JONES

The sermon of your life in tough times ministers to people more powerfully than the most eloquent speaker.

BILL BRIGHT

Every misfortune, every failure, every loss may be transformed. God has the power to transform all misfortunes into "God-sends."

MRS. CHARLES E. COWMAN

The only way to learn a strong faith is to endure great trials. I have learned my faith by standing firm amid the most severe of tests.

GEORGE MUELLER

If you learn to trust God with a child-like dependence on Him as your loving heavenly Father, no trouble can destroy you.

BILLY GRAHAM

Throughout history, when God's people found themselves facing impossible odds, they reminded themselves of God's limitless power.

BILL HYBELS

God will make obstacles serve His purpose.

MRS. CHARLES E. COWMAN

Adversity is not simply a tool. It is God's most effective tool for the advancement of our spiritual lives. The circumstances and events that we see as setbacks are oftentimes the very things that launch us into periods of intense spiritual growth. Once we begin to understand this, and accept it as a spiritual fact of life, adversity becomes easier to bear.

CHARLES STANLEY

MORE WISDOM FROM GOD'S WORD

I called to the Lord in my distress; I called to my God. From His temple He heard my voice.

2 SAMUEL 22:7 HCSB

I will be with you when you pass through the waters . . . when you walk through the fire . . . the flame will not burn you. For I the Lord your God, the Holy One of Israel, and your Savior.

ISAIAH 43:2-3 HCSB

Consider it a great joy, my brothers, whenever you experience various trials, knowing that the testing of your faith produces endurance. But endurance must do its complete work, so that you may be mature and complete, lacking nothing.

JAMES 1:2-4 HCSB

When you are in distress and all these things have happened to you, you will return to the Lord your God in later days and obey Him. He will not leave you, destroy you, or forget the covenant with your fathers that He swore to them by oath, because the Lord your God is a compassionate God.

DEUTERONOMY 4:30-31 HCSB

DREAM BIG

It takes courage to dream big dreams—dreams for yourself and your family. You'll discover the courage to dream big when you do three things: accept the past, trust God to handle the future, and make the most of the time He has given you today.

Are you excited about the opportunities of today and thrilled by the possibilities of tomorrow? Do you confidently expect God to lead you and yours to a place of abundance, peace, and joy? If you trust God's promises, you should believe that your future is intensely and eternally bright.

Today, promise yourself that you'll do your family (and the world) a king-sized favor by whole-heartedly pursuing your dreams. After all, no dreams are too big for God—not even yours. So start living—and dreaming—accordingly.

MORE GOOD IDEAS

Allow your dreams a place in your prayers and plans. God-given dreams can help you move into the future He is preparing for you.

BARBARA JOHNSON

Set goals so big that unless God helps you, you will be a miserable failure.

BILL BRIGHT

You cannot out-dream God.

JOHN ELDREDGE

A TIMELY TIP

If you're having tough times, don't hit the panic button and don't keep everything bottled up inside. Talk things over with people you can really trust. And if your troubles seem overwhelming, be willing to seek help—starting, of course, with your spouse and your pastor.

DEAR DAD,
On the Lines Below, Write Down Your Own Ideas About
Lessons You've Learned from Tough Times

And Finally . . .

YOU CAN INCREASE YOUR SUPPLY OF COURAGE BY SHARING IT.

CHAPTER 24

YOUR JOURNEY WITH GOD

I will instruct you and show you the way to go;
with My eye on you, I will give counsel.

—

PSALM 32:8 HCSB

Whether you realize it or not, Dad, you're on a journey with God. The Creator has things He wants you to do and places He wants you to go. The most important decision of your life is, of course, your commitment to accept Jesus Christ as your personal Lord and Savior. And, once your eternal destiny is secured, you will undoubtedly ask yourself the question "What now, Lord?" If you earnestly seek God's will for your life, you will find it . . . in time.

As you seek to discover God's path for your life, you should study His Holy Word and be ever watchful for His signs. You should associate with fellow Christians who will encourage your spiritual growth, and you should listen to that inner voice that speaks to you in the quiet moments of your daily devotionals.

Rest assured: God is here, and He intends to use you in wonderful, unexpected ways. He desires to lead you along a path of His choosing. Your challenge is to watch, to listen . . . and to follow.

MORE GREAT IDEAS ABOUT PURPOSE

Continually restate to yourself what the purpose of your life is.

OSWALD CHAMBERS

When God speaks to you through the Bible, prayer, circumstances, the church, or in some other way, he has a purpose in mind for your life.

HENRY BLACKABY AND CLAUDE KING

Without God, life has no purpose, and without purpose, life has no meaning.

RICK WARREN

Whatever purpose motivates your life, it must be something big enough and grand enough to make the investment worthwhile.

WARREN WIERSBE

The worst thing that laziness does is rob a man of spiritual purpose.

BILLY GRAHAM

God wants to revolutionize our lives—by showing us how knowing Him can be the most powerful force to help us become all we want to be.

BILL HYBELS

Their distress is due entirely to their deliberate determination to use themselves for a purpose other than God's.

OSWALD CHAMBERS

His life is our light—our purpose and meaning and reason for living.

ANNE GRAHAM LOTZ

Waiting means going about our assigned tasks, confident that God will provide the meaning and the conclusions.

EUGENE PETERSON

MORE WISDOM FROM GOD'S WORD

For it is God who is working among you both the willing and the working for His good purpose.

PHILIPPIANS 2:13 HCSB

We know that all things work together for the good of those who love God: those who are called according to His purpose.

ROMANS 8:28 HCSB

You reveal the path of life to me; in Your presence is abundant joy; in Your right hand are eternal pleasures.

PSALM 16:11 HCSB

Commit your activities to the Lord and your plans will be achieved.

PROVERBS 16:3 HCSB

In Him we were also made His inheritance, predestined according to the purpose of the One who works out everything in agreement with the decision of His will.

EPHESIANS 1:11 HCSB

MORE GOOD IDEAS

In the very place where God has put us, whatever its limitations, whatever kind of work it may be, we may indeed serve the Lord Christ.

ELISABETH ELLIOT

To be successful, one must grow to the point where he completely forgets himself; that is, loses himself in a great cause.

BOOKER T. WASHINGTON

Make your life a mission—not an intermission.

OLD SAYING

A TIMELY TIP

Ten years from now you will be somewhere—the question is where? You have the power to make that determination. And remember: it's not about earning a living; it's about designing a life.

DEAR DAD,
On the Lines Below, Write Down Your Own Ideas About Your Journey with God

_____

_____

_____

_____

_____

_____

_____

_____

_____

_____

_____

_____

_____

_____

_____

_____

_____

_____

_____

_____

CHAPTER 25

THE POWER OF PATIENCE

A patient spirit is better than a proud spirit.

—

ECCLESIASTES 7:8 HCSB

Family life demands patience . . . and lots of it! We live in imperfect homes inhabited by imperfect kids and their imperfect parents. Thank goodness family life doesn't have to be perfect to be wonderful!

Sometimes, we inherit troubles from other folks (some of whom live under our roofs, and some who don't). On other occasions, we create trouble for ourselves. In either case, what's required is patience.

So here's a reminder, Dad: the next time you find your patience tested to the limit by the limitations of others, remember that nobody who inhabits your world is perfect (including yourself). And remember that the less you manage to focus on other people's imperfections, the better for them and for you.

MORE GREAT IDEAS ABOUT
PATIENCE

You can't step in front of God and not get in trouble. When He says, "Go three steps," don't go four.

CHARLES STANLEY

God is more patient with us than we are with ourselves.

MAX LUCADO

If God is diligent, surely we ought to be diligent in doing our duty to Him. Think how patient and diligent God has been to us!

OSWALD CHAMBERS

In all negotiations of difficulties, a man may not look to sow and reap at once. He must prepare his business and so ripen it by degrees.

FRANCIS BACON

In the Bible, patience is not a passive acceptance of circumstances. It is a courageous perseverance in the face of suffering and difficulty.

WARREN WIERSBE

The next time you're disappointed, don't panic. Don't give up. Just be patient and let God remind you he's still in control.

MAX LUCADO

Grass that is here today and gone tomorrow does not require much time to mature. A big oak tree that lasts for generations requires much more time to grow and mature. God is concerned about your life through eternity. Allow Him to take all the time He needs to shape you for His purposes. Larger assignments will require longer periods of preparation.

HENRY BLACKABY

Our challenge is to wait in faith for the day of God's favor and salvation.

JIM CYMBALA

Wisdom always waits for the right time to act, while emotion always pushes for action right now.

JOYCE MEYER

How do you wait upon the Lord? First you must learn to sit at His feet and take time to listen to His words.

KAY ARTHUR

MORE WISDOM FROM GOD'S WORD

Love is patient; love is kind.

1 CORINTHIANS 13:4 HCSB

Therefore the Lord is waiting to show you mercy, and is rising up to show you compassion, for the Lord is a just God. Happy are all who wait patiently for Him.

ISAIAH 30:18 HCSB

Be gentle to everyone, able to teach, and patient.

2 TIMOTHY 2:23 HCSB

Now we exhort you, brethren, warn those who are unruly, comfort the fainthearted, uphold the weak, be patient with all.

1 THESSALONIANS 5:14 NKJV

My dearly loved brothers, understand this: everyone must be quick to hear, slow to speak, and slow to anger, for man's anger does not accomplish God's righteousness.

JAMES 1:19-20 HCSB

MORE GOOD IDEAS

Genius is nothing more than a greater aptitude for patience.

BEN FRANKLIN

A man watches his pear tree day after day, impatient for the ripening of the fruit. Let him attempt to force the ripening fruit, and he may spoil both fruit and tree. But, let him patiently wait, and the ripe pear, at length, falls into his lap.

ABRAHAM LINCOLN

Delay is preferable to error.

THOMAS JEFFERSON

A TIMELY TIP

Do you want your family members to be patient with you? Then you must do the same for them. Never expect other people to be more patient with you than you are with them.

DEAR DAD,
On the Lines Below, Write Down Your Own Ideas About
The Power of Patience

CHAPTER 26

FATHERS WHO TEACH

Set an example of good works yourself,
with integrity and dignity in your teaching.

—

TITUS 2:7 HCSB

A father's responsibilities are profound. Being a godly parent in today's difficult world requires insight, discipline, patience, prayer, and a willingness to teach.

Do you sincerely seek to leave a lasting legacy for generations to come? If so, you must start by teaching your children the ways and the Word of God. And remember always that your most enduring lessons are not only the ones you teach with words; they are also the ones you teach by example. When you obey God's commandments and trust His promises, your life will be a shining lesson for your children . . . and for theirs.

MORE GREAT IDEAS ABOUT TEACHING

Begin very early to instruct a child on the true values of life: love for all mankind, kindness, integrity, trustworthiness, truthfulness, and devotion to God.

JAMES DOBSON

If a teacher fascinates with his doctrine, his teaching never came from God. The teacher who came from God is the one who clears the way for Jesus and keeps it clear.

OSWALD CHAMBERS

God often keeps us on the path by guiding us through the counsel of friends and trusted spiritual advisors.

BILL HYBELS

The next best thing to being wise oneself is to live in a circle of those who are.

C. S. LEWIS

It is desirable that children be kind, appreciative and pleasant. Those qualities should be taught and not hoped for.

JAMES DOBSON

Training is not telling, not teaching, not commanding, but something higher than all of these. It is not only telling a child what to do, but it is also showing him how to do it and seeing that it is done.

ANDREW MURRAY

The effective mentor strives to help a man or woman discover what they can be in Christ and then holds them accountable to become that person.

HOWARD HENDRICKS

Yes, the Spirit was sent to be our Counselor. Yes, Jesus speaks to us personally. But often he works through another human being.

JOHN ELDREDGE

Their little minds had a thousand hands reaching and grabbing for everything they could see (not unlike their physical hands). A parent-teacher's job is to guide as much as possible what the hands of their minds grab and store.

BETH MOORE

Leading our children to Christ should be at the top of our mission and prayer list.

ANNIE CHAPMAN

MORE WISDOM FROM GOD'S WORD

Teach a youth about the way he should go; even when he is old he will not depart from it.

PROVERBS 22:6 HCSB

According to the grace given to us, we have different gifts: If prophecy, use it according to the standard of faith; if service, in service; if teaching, in teaching; if exhorting, in exhortation; giving, with generosity; leading, with diligence; showing mercy, with cheerfulness.

ROMANS 12:6-8 HCSB

Be conscientious about yourself and your teaching; persevere in these things, for by doing this you will save both yourself and your hearers.

1 TIMOTHY 4:13 HCSB

Let the word of Christ dwell in you richly in all wisdom, teaching and admonishing one another in psalms and hymns and spiritual songs, singing with grace in your hearts to the Lord.

COLOSSIANS 3:16 NKJV

MORE GOOD IDEAS

The best way to keep your wisdom fresh is to give it away every day.

OLD SAYING

People need to be reminded more often than they need to be instructed.

SAMUEL JOHNSON

If we work in marble, it will perish; if we work upon brass, time will efface it; if we rear temples, they will crumble into dust; but if we work upon immortal minds and instill in them just principles, we are then engraving upon tablets which no time will efface, but will brighten and brighten to all eternity.

DANIEL WEBSTER

A TIMELY TIP

Helping our children understand the fundamental truths of Christian living requires time, and lots of it. Our children are always learning. As parents, we must ensure that they are learning from us.

DEAR DAD,
On the Lines Below, Write Down Your Own Ideas About
Important Lessons to Teach

CHAPTER 27

FATHERS WHO TRUST GOD'S WORD

All Scripture is inspired by God and is profitable for teaching, for rebuking, for correcting, for training in righteousness, so that the man of God may be complete, equipped for every good work.

—

2 TIMOTHY 3:16-17 HCSB

Matthew 4:4 teaches us that, "Man shall not live by bread alone but by every word that proceedeth out of the mouth of God" (KJV). As believers, we must study the Bible and meditate upon its meaning for our lives. Otherwise, we deprive ourselves of a priceless gift from our Creator.

God's Holy Word is unlike any other book. The Bible is a roadmap for life here on earth and for life eternal. As Christians, we are called upon to study God's Holy Word, to follow its commandments, and to share its Good News with the world.

Jonathan Edwards advised, "Be assiduous in reading the Holy Scriptures. This is the fountain whence all knowledge in divinity must be derived. Therefore let not this treasure lie by you neglected." God's Holy Word is, indeed, a priceless, one-of-a-kind treasure, and a passing acquaintance with the Good Book is insufficient for Christians who seek to obey God's Word and to understand His will. After all, man does not live by bread alone . . .

MORE GREAT IDEAS ABOUT
GOD'S WORD

Nobody ever outgrows Scripture; the book widens and deepens with our years.

C. H. SPURGEON

When you meet with God, open the Bible. Don't rely on your memory; rely on those printed pages.

CHARLES SWINDOLL

Faith is the virtue that enables us to believe and obey the Word of God, for faith comes from hearing and hearing from the Word of God (Romans 10:17).

FRANKLIN GRAHAM

It takes calm, thoughtful, prayerful meditation on the Word to extract its deepest nourishment.

VANCE HAVNER

Cling to the whole Bible, not to part of it. A man is not going to do much with a broken sword.

D. L. MOODY

My meditation and study have shown me that, like God, His Word is holy, everlasting, absolutely true, powerful, personally fair, and never changing.

BILL BRIGHT

Words fail to express my love for this holy Book, my gratitude for its author, for His love and goodness. How shall I thank him for it?

LOTTIE MOON

Meditating upon His Word will inevitably bring peace of mind, strength of purpose, and power for living.

BILL BRIGHT

The Holy Spirit is the Spirit of Truth, which means He always works according to and through the Word of God whether you feel Him or not.

ANNE GRAHAM LOTZ

MORE WISDOM FROM GOD'S WORD

For I am not ashamed of the gospel, because it is God's power for salvation to everyone who believes.

ROMANS 1:16 HCSB

Man shall not live by bread alone, but by every word that proceeds from the mouth of God.

MATTHEW 4:4 NKJV

Heaven and earth will pass away, but My words will never pass away.

MATTHEW 24:35 HCSB

For the word of God is living and effective and sharper than any two-edged sword, penetrating as far as to divide soul, spirit, joints, and marrow; it is a judge of the ideas and thoughts of the heart.

HEBREWS 4:12 HCSB

Your word is a lamp for my feet and a light on my path.

PSALM 119:105 HCSB

KEEP GROWING SPIRITUALLY

Your relationship with God is ongoing; it unfolds day by day, and it offers countless opportunities to grow closer to Him . . . or not. As each new day unfolds, you are confronted with a wide range of decisions: how you will behave, where you will direct your thoughts, with whom you will associate, and what you will choose to worship. These choices, along with many others like them, are yours and yours alone. How you choose determines how your relationship with God will unfold.

Are you continuing to grow in your love and knowledge of the Lord, or are you "satisfied" with the current state of your spiritual health? Hopefully, you're determined to make yourself a growing Christian. Your Savior deserves no less, and neither, by the way, do you.

MORE GOOD IDEAS

Growth takes place in quietness, in hidden ways, in silence and solitude. The process is not accessible to observation.

EUGENE PETERSON

We often become mentally and spiritually barren because we're so busy.

FRANKLIN GRAHAM

The vigor of our spiritual lives will be in exact proportion to the place held by the Bible in our lives and in our thoughts.

GEORGE MUELLER

A TIMELY TIP

Charles Swindoll writes, "There are four words I wish we would never forget, and they are, 'God keeps his word.'" And remember: When it comes to studying God's Word, school is always in session.

DEAR DAD,

On the Lines Below, Write Down Your Own Ideas About
The Importance of Studying and Trusting God's Word

AND FINALLY . . .

IF YOUR BIBLE IS FALLING APART,
CHANCES ARE YOUR LIFE
IS STAYING TOGETHER.

CHAPTER 28

CELEBRATING LIFE

Rejoice in the Lord always. I will say it again: Rejoice!

—

PHILIPPIANS 4:4 HCSB

What is the best day to celebrate life? This one! Today and every day should be a day of prayer and celebration as we consider the Good News of God's free gift: salvation through Jesus Christ.

What do you expect from the day ahead? Are you expecting God to do wonderful things, or are you living beneath a cloud of apprehension and doubt? The familiar words of Psalm 118:24 remind us of a profound yet simple truth: "This is the day which the LORD hath made" (KJV). Our duty, as believers, is to rejoice in God's marvelous creation.

For Christians, every day begins and ends with God and His Son. Christ came to this earth to give us abundant life and eternal salvation. We give thanks to our Maker when we treasure each day. May we use our time here on earth to serve God, to celebrate His marvelous gifts, and to share His Good News with the world.

MORE GREAT IDEAS ABOUT
JOY

We all sin by needlessly disobeying the apostolic injunction to rejoice.

C. S. LEWIS

The ability to rejoice in any situation is a sign of spiritual maturity.

BILLY GRAHAM

Joy is the direct result of having God's perspective on our daily lives and the effect of loving our Lord enough to obey His commands and trust His promises.

BILL BRIGHT

Joy is the heart's harmonious response to the Lord's song of love.

A. W. TOZER

Today you will encounter God's creation. When you see the beauty around you, let each detail remind you to lift your head in praise.

MAX LUCADO

A life of intimacy with God is characterized by joy.

OSWALD CHAMBERS

Rejoice, the Lord is King; Your Lord and King adore! Rejoice, give thanks and sing and triumph evermore.

CHARLES WESLEY

Gratitude changes the pangs of memory into a tranquil joy.

DIETRICH BONHOEFFER

Jesus did not promise to change the circumstances around us. He promised great peace and pure joy to those who would learn to believe that God actually controls all things.

CORRIE TEN BOOM

If you're a thinking Christian, you will be a joyful Christian.

MARIE T. FREEMAN

MORE WISDOM FROM GOD'S WORD

Make me to hear joy and gladness.

PSALM 51:8 KJV

Now I am coming to You, and I speak these things in the world so that they may have My joy completed in them.

JOHN 17:13 HCSB

So you also have sorrow now. But I will see you again. Your hearts will rejoice, and no one will rob you of your joy.

JOHN 16:22 HCSB

Weeping may spend the night, but there is joy in the morning.

PSALM 30:5 HCSB

Glory in His holy name; let the hearts of those rejoice who seek the Lord! Seek the Lord and His strength; seek His face evermore!

1 CHRONICLES 16:10-11 NKJV

SHARE YOUR ENTHUSIASM

Genuine, heartfelt Christianity is contagious. If you enjoy a life-altering relationship with God, that relationship will have an impact on others—perhaps a profound impact.

Are you genuinely excited about your faith? And do you make your enthusiasm known to those around you? Or are you a "silent ambassador" for Christ? God's preference is clear: He intends that you stand before others and proclaim your faith.

Does Christ reign over your life? Then share your testimony and your excitement. The world needs both.

MORE GOOD IDEAS

Enthusiasm, like the flu, is contagious—we get it from one another.

BARBARA JOHNSON

Wherever you are, be all there. Live to the hilt every situation you believe to be the will of God.

JIM ELLIOT

One of the great needs in the church today is for every Christian to become enthusiastic about his faith in Jesus Christ.

BILLY GRAHAM

A TIMELY TIP

Joy is contagious: Remember that a joyful family starts with joyful parents.

DEAR DAD,
On the Lines Below, Write Down Your Own Ideas About The Value of Enthusiasm

_____

_____

_____

_____

_____

_____

_____

_____

_____

_____

_____

_____

_____

_____

_____

_____

_____

_____

_____

_____

_____

AND FINALLY . . .

TODAY IS A GIFT FROM GOD.
THAT'S WHY IT IS CALLED "THE PRESENT."

CHAPTER 29

THE IMPORTANCE OF LAUGHTER

There is an occasion for everything, and a time for every activity under heaven . . . a time to weep and a time to laugh; a time to mourn and a time to dance.

—

ECCLESIASTES 3:1,4 HCSB

Fatherhood is no laughing matter; it should be taken very seriously, up to a point. But no father's responsibilities should be so burdensome that he forgets to laugh. Laughter is medicine for the soul, but sometimes, amid the stresses of the day, we forget to take our medicine. Instead of viewing our world with a mixture of optimism and humor, we allow worries and distractions to rob us of the joy that God intends for our lives.

If your heart is heavy, open the door of your soul to Christ. He will give you peace and joy. And, if you already have the joy of Christ in your heart, share it freely, just as Christ freely shared His joy with you.

As you go about your daily activities, approach life with a smile on your lips and hope in your heart. And laugh every chance you get. After all, God created laughter for a reason . . . and Father indeed knows best. So laugh!

MORE GREAT IDEAS ABOUT LAUGHTER

The people whom I have seen succeed best in life have always been cheerful and hopeful people who went about their business with a smile on their faces.

CHARLES KINGSLEY

If you want people to feel comfortable around you, to enjoy being with you, then learn to laugh at yourself and find humor in life's little mishaps.

DENNIS SWANBERG

A little comic relief in a discussion does no harm, however serious the topic may be. (In my own experience the funniest things have occurred in the gravest and most sincere conversations.)

C. S. LEWIS

I think everybody ought to be a laughing Christian. I'm convinced that there's just one place where there's not any laughter, and that's hell.

JERRY CLOWER

Christ can put a spring in your step and a thrill in your heart. Optimism and cheerfulness are products of knowing Christ.

BILLY GRAHAM

Humor ought to be consecrated and used for the cause of Christ.

C. H. SPURGEON

It is pleasing to the dear God whenever you rejoice or laugh from the bottom of your heart.

MARTIN LUTHER

Laughter is to life what shock absorbers are to automobiles. It won't take the potholes out of the road, but it sure makes the ride smoother.

BARBARA JOHNSON

Humor is a prelude to faith, and laughter is the beginning of prayer.

REINHOLD NIEBUHR

Mirth is God's medicine. Everybody ought to bathe in it.

HENRY WARD BEECHER

MORE WISDOM FROM GOD'S WORD

Oh, clap your hands, all you peoples! Shout to God with the voice of triumph!

PSALM 47:1 NKJV

A joyful heart makes a face cheerful.

PROVERBS 15:13 HCSB

The Lord reigns; let the earth rejoice.

PSALM 97:1 NKJV

I have spoken these things to you so that My joy may be in you and your joy may be complete.

JOHN 15:11 HCSB

Blessed are you who are hungry now, because you will be filled. Blessed are you who weep now, because you will laugh.

LUKE 6:21 HCSB

MORE GOOD IDEAS

Laughter is the sun that drives winter from the human face.

VICTOR HUGO

Trouble knocked on the door, but, hearing a laugh within, hurried away.

BEN FRANKLIN

Laugh and the world laughs with you.

ELLA WHEELER WILCOX

A TIMELY TIP

Get the whole family involved: Laughter is the icing on the cake of family life, and everybody in your clan deserves a slice.

DEAR DAD,
On the Lines Below, Write Down Your Own Ideas About
The Need to Laugh with Life

_____

_____

_____

_____

_____

_____

_____

_____

_____

_____

_____

_____

_____

_____

_____

_____

_____

_____

_____

CHAPTER 30

THE POWER OF POSITIVE THOUGHTS

But if we look forward to something we don't have yet,
we must wait patiently and confidently.

—

ROMANS 8:25 NLT

Of course you've heard the saying, "Life is what you make it." And although that statement may seem very trite, it's also very true. You can choose a life filled to the brim with frustration and fear, or you can choose a life of abundance and peace. That choice is up to you—and only you—and it depends, to a surprising extent, upon your attitude.

What's your attitude today, Dad? And what's the prevailing attitude of the people who live under your roof? Are you fearful, angry, bored, or worried? Are you pessimistic, perplexed, pained, and perturbed? If so, it's time for an attitude adjustment.

God created you (and yours) in His own image, and He wants you (and yours) to experience joy, contentment, peace, and abundance. But, God will not force you to experience these things; you must claim them for yourselves. And when is the best time to start reaping the rewards of positive thinking? Right now, of course, if not sooner.

MORE GREAT IDEAS ABOUT OPTIMISM

It is a remarkable thing that some of the most optimistic and enthusiastic people you will meet are those who have been through intense suffering.

WARREN WIERSBE

The popular idea of faith is of a certain obstinate optimism: the hope, tenaciously held in the face of trouble, that the universe is fundamentally friendly and things may get better.

J. I. PACKER

The essence of optimism is that it takes no account of the present, but it is a source of inspiration, of vitality, and of hope. Where others have resigned, it enables a man to hold his head high, to claim the future for himself, and not abandon it to his enemy.

DIETRICH BONHOEFFER

The people whom I have seen succeed best in life have always been cheerful and hopeful people who went about their business with a smile on their faces.

CHARLES KINGSLEY

Keep your feet on the ground, but let your heart soar as high as it will. Refuse to be average or to surrender to the chill of your spiritual environment.

A. W. TOZER

If our hearts have been attuned to God through an abiding faith in Christ, the result will be joyous optimism and good cheer.

BILLY GRAHAM

Oh, remember this: There is never a time when we may not hope in God. Whatever our necessities, however great our difficulties, and though to all appearance help is impossible, yet our business is to hope in God, and it will be found that it is not in vain.

GEORGE MUELLER

Troubles we bear trustfully can bring us a fresh vision of God and a new outlook on life, an outlook of peace and hope.

BILLY GRAHAM

MORE WISDOM FROM GOD'S WORD

Make me hear joy and gladness.

PSALM 51:8 NKJV

My cup runs over. Surely goodness and mercy shall follow me all the days of my life; and I will dwell in the house of the Lord forever.

PSALM 23:5-6 NKJV

I can do everything through him that gives me strength.

PHILIPPIANS 4:13 NIV

For God has not given us a spirit of fear, but of power and of love and of a sound mind.

2 TIMOTHY 1:7 NLT

Be cheerful no matter what; pray all the time; thank God no matter what happens. This is the way God wants you who belong to Christ Jesus to live.

1 THESSALONIANS 5:16-18 MSG

DEFEATING PESSIMISM

Pessimism is intellectual poison. And negativity has the power to harm your heart if you let it. So if you've allowed negative thoughts to creep into your mind and heart, here's your assignment: Start spending more time thinking about your blessings and less time fretting about your hardships.

This day, like every other, is a gift from God, filled to the brim with possibilities. But persistent pessimistic thoughts can rob you of the energy you need to accomplish the most important tasks on your to-do list. So today, be careful to direct your thoughts toward things positive. And while you're at it, take time to thank the Giver of all things good for gifts that are, in truth, far too numerous to count.

MORE GOOD IDEAS

To lose heart is to lose everything.

JOHN ELDREDGE

We never get anywhere—nor do our conditions and circumstances change—when we look at the dark side of life.

MRS. CHARLES E. COWMAN

A pessimist is someone who believes that when her cup runneth over she'll need a mop.

BARBARA JOHNSON

A TIMELY TIP

If your thoughts tend toward the negative end of the spectrum, redirect them. How? You can start by counting your blessings and by thanking your Father in heaven. And while you're at it, train yourself to begin thinking thoughts that are more rational, more accepting, and more upbeat (Philippians 4:8) . . . for your children's sake.

DEAR DAD,
On the Lines Below, Write Down Your Own Ideas About The Need for Optimism

_____

_____

_____

_____

_____

_____

_____

_____

_____

_____

_____

_____

_____

_____

_____

_____

_____

_____

_____

_____

AND FINALLY . . .

PARENTS CAN TELL BUT NEVER TEACH,
UNTIL THEY PRACTICE WHAT THEY PREACH.

CHAPTER 31

THE POWER OF PERSEVERANCE

Though a righteous man falls seven times,
he will get up, but the wicked will stumble into ruin.

—

PROVERBS 24:16 HCSB

Someone once said, "Life is a marathon, not a sprint." The same can be said for fatherhood. Fatherhood requires courage, perseverance, determination, and, of course, an unending supply of love.

As you continue to search for purpose in everyday life (while, at the same time, balancing all your paternal responsibilities), you'll encounter your fair share of roadblocks and stumbling blocks. These situations require courage, patience, and above all, perseverance. As an example of perfect perseverance, we Christians need look no further than our Savior, Jesus Christ.

Jesus, finished what He began. Despite the torture He endured, despite the shame of the cross, Jesus was steadfast in His faithfulness to God. We, too, must remain faithful, especially during times of hardship.

Are you tired? Ask God for strength. Are you discouraged? Believe in His promises. Are you frustrated or fearful? Pray as if everything depended upon God, and work as if everything depended upon you. With God's help, you will find the strength to be the kind of dad who makes your Heavenly Father beam with pride.

MORE GREAT IDEAS ABOUT PERSEVERANCE

Battles are won in the trenches, in the grit and grime of courageous determination; they are won day by day in the arena of life.

CHARLES SWINDOLL

You cannot persevere unless there is a trial in your life. There can be no victories without battles; there can be no peaks without valleys. If you want the blessing, you must be prepared to carry the burden and fight the battle. God has to balance privileges with responsibilities, blessings with burdens, or else you and I will become spoiled, pampered children.

WARREN WIERSBE

Press on. Obstacles are seldom the same size tomorrow as they are today.

ROBERT SCHULLER

Perseverance is more than endurance. It is endurance combined with absolute assurance and certainty that what we are looking for is going to happen.

OSWALD CHAMBERS

All rising to a great place is by a winding stair.

FRANCIS BACON

Only the man who follows the command of Jesus single-mindedly and unresistingly lets his yoke rest upon him, finds his burden easy, and under its gentle pressure receives the power to persevere in the right way.

DIETRICH BONHOEFFER

By perseverance the snail reached the ark.

C. H. SPURGEON

As we find that it is not easy to persevere in this being "alone with God," we begin to realize that it is because we are not "wholly for God." God has a right to demand that He should have us completely for Himself.

ANDREW MURRAY

MORE WISDOM FROM GOD'S WORD

Let us not become weary in doing good, for at the proper time we will reap a harvest if we do not give up.

GALATIANS 6:9 NIV

For you have need of endurance, so that when you have done the will of God, you may receive what was promised.

HEBREWS 10:36 NASB

Thanks be to God! He gives us the victory through our Lord Jesus Christ. Therefore, my dear brothers, stand firm. Let nothing move you. Always give yourselves fully to the work of the Lord, because you know that your labor in the Lord is not in vain.

1 CORINTHIANS 15:57-58 NIV

Be diligent that ye may be found of him in peace, without spot, and blameless.

2 PETER 3:14 KJV

Have you not known? Have you not heard? The everlasting God, the Lord, the Creator of the ends of the earth, neither faints nor is weary. His understanding is unsearchable. He gives power to the weak, and to those who have no might He increases strength.

ISAIAH 40:28-29 NKJV

GOD'S PROTECTION

Have you ever faced challenges that seemed too big to handle? Have you ever faced big problems that, despite your best efforts, simply could not be solved? If so, you know how uncomfortable it is to feel helpless in the face of difficult circumstances. Thankfully, even when there's nowhere else to turn, you can turn your thoughts and prayers to God, and He will respond.

God's hand uplifts those who turn their hearts and prayers to Him. Count yourself among that number. When you do, you can live courageously and joyfully, knowing that "this too will pass"—but that God's love for you will not. And you can draw strength from the knowledge that you are a marvelous creation, loved, protected, and uplifted by the ever-present hand of God.

MORE GOOD IDEAS

Faith is not merely you holding on to God—it is God holding on to you.

E. STANLEY JONES

The last and greatest lesson that the soul has to learn is the fact that God, and God alone, is enough for all its needs. This is the lesson that all His dealings with us are meant to teach; and this is the crowning discovery of our whole Christian life. God is enough!

HANNAH WHITALL SMITH

Only God can move mountains, but faith and prayer can move God.

E. M. BOUNDS

A TIMELY TIP

When you are in the center of God's will, you are in the center of God's protection.

DEAR DAD,
On the Lines Below, Write Down Your Own Ideas About The Power of Perseverance

_____

_____

_____

_____

_____

_____

_____

_____

_____

_____

_____

_____

_____

_____

_____

_____

_____

_____

_____

_____

_____

AND FINALLY . . .

Little strokes fell great oaks.

—

POOR RICHARD'S ALMANAC

CHAPTER 32

GIVING THANKS FOR GOD'S BLESSINGS

You will show me the path of life;
in Your presence is fullness of joy;
at Your right hand are pleasures forevermore.

—

PSALM 16:11 NKJV

Because you are a father, you have been specially blessed by God. God has given you blessings that are too numerous to count. Your blessings include life, family, freedom, friends, talents, and possessions, for starters. But, your greatest blessing—a gift that is yours for the asking—is God's gift of salvation through Christ Jesus.

The gifts you receive from God are multiplied when you share them with others. Today, give thanks to God for your blessings and demonstrate your gratitude by sharing those blessings with your family and with the world.

MORE GREAT IDEAS ABOUT GOD'S BLESSINGS

Grace is an outrageous blessing bestowed freely on a totally undeserving recipient.

BILL HYBELS

God's love for His children is unconditional, no strings attached. But, God's blessings on our lives do come with a condition—obedience. If we are to receive the fullness of God's blessings, we must obey Him and keep His commandments.

JIM GALLERY

With the goodness of God to desire our highest welfare and the wisdom of God to plan it, what do we lack? Surely we are the most favored of all creatures.

A. W. TOZER

The Christian life is motivated, not by a list of do's and don'ts, but by the gracious outpouring of God's love and blessing.

ANNE GRAHAM LOTZ

It is when we give ourselves to be a blessing that we can specially count on the blessing of God.

ANDREW MURRAY

Get rich quick! Count your blessings!

ANONYMOUS

Blessings can either humble us and draw us closer to God or allow us to become full of pride and self-sufficiency.

JIM CYMBALA

God blesses us in spite of our lives and not because of our lives.

MAX LUCADO

God is always far more willing to give us good things than we are anxious to have them.

CATHERINE MARSHALL

MORE WISDOM FROM GOD'S WORD

Blessed is a man who endures trials, because when he passes the test he will receive the crown of life that He has promised to those who love Him.

JAMES 1:12 HCSB

I will make them and the area around My hill a blessing: I will send down showers in their season—showers of blessing.

EZEKIEL 34:26 HCSB

The Lord bless you and keep you; the Lord make His face shine upon you, and be gracious to you.

NUMBERS 6:24-25 NKJV

I will make you a great nation; I will bless you and make your name great; and you shall be a blessing. I will bless those who bless you, and I will curse him who curses you; and in you all the families of the earth shall be blessed.

GENESIS 12:2-3 NKJV

Come to terms with God and be at peace; in this way good will come to you.

JOB 22:21 HCSB

FOR GOD SO LOVED THE WORLD

How much does God love you? To answer that question, you need only to look at the cross. God's love for you is so great that He sent His only Son to this earth to die for your sins and to offer you the priceless gift of eternal life.

You must decide whether or not to accept God's gift. Will you ignore it or embrace it? Will you return it or neglect it? Will you invite Christ to dwell in the center of your heart, or will you relegate Him to a position of lesser importance? The decision is yours, and so are the consequences. So choose wisely . . . and choose today.

MORE GOOD IDEAS

Teach us to set our hopes on heaven, to hold firmly to the promise of eternal life, so that we can withstand the struggles and storms of this world.

MAX LUCADO

And because we know Christ is alive, we have hope for the present and hope for life beyond the grave.

BILLY GRAHAM

Once a man is united to God, how could he not live forever? Once a man is separated from God, what can he do but wither and die?

C. S. LEWIS

A TIMELY TIP

God offers you a priceless gift: the gift of eternal life. If you have not already done so, accept God's gift today—tomorrow may be too late.

DEAR DAD,
On the Lines Below, Write Down Your Own Ideas About God's Eternal Gifts

And Finally . . .

BIBLE:

Basic
Instructions
Before
Leaving
Earth